The English Programme

Language

This book was made by Steve Goldenberg, Peter Griffiths, John Lee and Margaret Sandra.

The TV programmes and teachers' notes on which this book is based were produced by Alan Horrox, David Stafford, and Peter Tabern. The publications officer was Lesley Sutch and the programme adviser was Professor Harold Rosen.

Contents

1 **Which English?** – *Dialects, accents and status*
English, English everywhere p**5**
Social groups and standard English p**9**
Change in group, change in language p**13**
Local dialects and accents p**16**

2 **Language rules!** – *Making meanings*
First kinds of talk p**20**
Different kinds of talk p**23**
Sharing meanings p**26**
Different meanings p**28**
Changing meanings p**31**

3 **Says who?** – *Language and power*
Different situation, different kind of talk p**34**
Power talks p**36**
Getting your own way p**38**
Fitting in – or breaking the rules p**41**

4 **True stories** – *Understanding narratives*
Stories all round p**45**
Some features of all stories p**48**
A new world and a point of view p**52**
Limits on stories p**53**
Making a meaning p**55**

5 **Cold print** – *Reading and writing*
The need to read p**57**
Different histories, different needs p**63**
Literature is knowledge p**67**

Language

This book covers the same subjects as five television programmes about language made by Thames Television. If you read through it, discuss it and work on its activities with friends, you should be able to understand the programmes much better.

You should also have learnt a lot about the ways in which the English language is used as a very powerful force in Britain, a force which affects all of us every day. It is used to tell us who we are, and how we should behave, who to look up to, who to look down on, who we should love, who we should hate, who we may talk to and who we may not.

If we become more aware of how this happens, then we can understand ourselves better, and understand how we can question these things.

You can start by questioning the ideas in this book.

Think of other examples to back up the points you agree with and to back up your own ideas when you disagree.

Each chapter is meant to be read as a connected set of ideas, but it is possible to concentrate more on some sections than others.

Most of the book is printed in three styles. **The commentary, written by the editors, is printed in bold, like this sentence.** It includes most of the main ideas about language that are being offered to you in the book. Extracts and examples from other writers are in medium print – like this sentence. And activities for you to work on, to practise what you know and what you have learnt about language, are printed in bold in square boxes – as at the top of p.28.

Some of the pieces of writing try to give you an impression of the accent of the man or woman speaking, eg the Scot who reads the news in Tom Leonard's poem on p.12. This is done usually by missing letters out (such as *'im* for *him* in a Cockney accent) or by adding letters (*bwoy* for *boy* in a Jamaican accent). A lot of missed letters or added letters make it harder to read, but we hope you won't give up. Because, mostly, these accents are the accents of working people – the very people whose speech is not often presented as worthy of serious attention.

A summary of the contents

1 **Which English?** is about the importance of standard English in the world today and how it is used by some people to make local accents and dialects.

2 **Language rules!** describes how everybody develops the ability to speak in many different ways, while being limited at the same time by the shared meanings already built into the language we learn.

3 **Says who?** examines how language is affected by relationships between people and by the situations they find themselves in.

4 **True stories** looks at some characteristics of narrative and at some of the factors that influence the production of oral and written stories.

5 **Cold print** shows the importance of writing and reading for all of us nowadays, both for individuals and communities.

Acknowledgements to the following for use of their copyright illustrations:

Jean Mohr (p.5), *Encyclopaedia Britannica* (p.6), Claudius Ceccon and IDAC (Institute of Cultural Action) (p.8), *Spare Rib* (p.11), *Listener* (p.11), Universal Pictorial Press (p.13), Janine Wiedel (p.15, 44), John Topham Picture Library (p.17), Richard and Sally Greenhill, Margaret Murray, Popperfotos (p.22, 43), Eyre and Spottiswoode Ltd and Graham Morris (p. 24), *Time Out* (p.24), Mel Calman (p.27), Gollancz Ltd (p.33), *Financial Times* (p.34), *Evening Standard* (p.37, 41, 70), TV Handbook (Scan) for original of cartoon 'Television' (p.36), Socialist Workers Press (p.39, 68), Mary Evans Picture Library (p.51), BBC (p.52), Granada TV (p.53), Keystone (p.54), Radio Times Hulton Picture Library (p.42, 63), St Bride Printing Library (p.64), John Griffiths (p.65), London Transport Executive (p.66).
Every effort has been made to trace ownership of copyright. The publishers would be grateful to hear from copyright holders whom we have been unable to contact.

**Thames Television Ltd.,
306 Euston Road, London NW1 3BB**

In association with

**Hutchinson & Co. (Publishers) Ltd.
3 Fitzroy Square, London W1P 6JD**

London Melbourne Sydney Auckland Wellington Johannesburg and agencies throughout the world

Printed in Great Britain by Eyre & Spottiswoode Ltd

ISBN 0 09 140511 4

1 Which English?

English, English everywhere

The people on this planet speak thousands of different languages between them. Nobody knows all of them. If you've just arrived in a foreign country where you don't speak the language, it can be a frightening and bewildering experience. Here is a description of some migrant workers from small villages in Turkey arriving in a big city in West Germany. It is their first time away from home.

. . . They are led off the platform to a reception centre. Behind the sound of their own excited speech comes the clipped noise of an incomprehensible language. The loudspeakers speak their own language but as if linen was tied tight across the mouth of the woman speaking. They would prefer it not to be a woman. Who is she? Who is telling her what to say? The written letters of the other language are jumbled together to make silent sounds.

SCHOKOLADE IST GUT!

The silence is his. Whatever they are saying, he, with the silent sounds in his head, is going to nod.

Everything looks new. The way people walk and move about at different levels, as though each level was unmistakably the ground. The surfaces walked on, or touched. The unusual sound which a usual movement makes. The seamless joints between things. Even glass looks different here, thicker and less brittle. The newness of the substance of things combines with the incomprehensibility of the language.

polystyrene	lön
övertid	cellulose acetate
epok	arbetstillstand
dödsfall	glass fibre

A Seventh Man JOHN BERGER and JEAN MOHR (Penguin 1975)

People who speak English don't often feel quite so lost as these men do, because there is often somebody else around who speaks it. English is spoken more widely than any other language. It is used, for one reason or another, in every country in the world.

It is unreasonable to regard any language as the property of a particular nation, and with no language is it more unreasonable than with English. This is not to say that English is used by a greater number of speakers than any other language: it is easily outstripped in this respect by Chinese. But it is the most *international* of languages. A Dane and a Dutchman meeting casually in Rome will almost automatically find themselves conversing in English. The crew of a Russian airliner approaching Cairo will use English to ask for landing instructions. Malayan lecturers use it as the medium of instruction when addressing their Malayan students in Kuala Lumpur.

The Use of English R. QUIRK (Longman 1967)

You may wonder why English is spoken in every corner of the globe. The answer is that for 400 years, from the sixteenth century onwards, British rulers sent armies, explorers, and missionaries to take over other countries. Only 40 years ago Britain had control over all these areas.

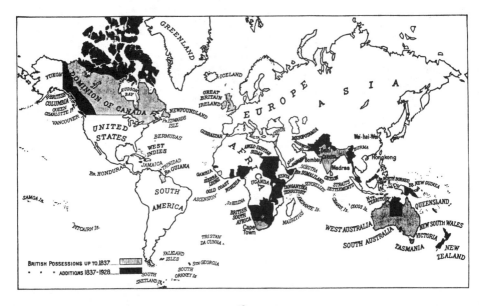

6

Its industrial and scientific development also gave Britain importance in the world. As Britain became a top nation, so English became top language. Even today, the English language is still powerful in the countries it used to control – the old British Empire. Here a Pakistani teenager describes how he used English to seem superior in Pakistan:

I went to the bank – right – and – my grandfather, he says, 'if you speak English, you know, we might get better terms.' OK so I dressed up properly, you know, dressing is very important in Pakistan. They look at you and they can tell what sort of person you are from your dressing, right? Now – they can! – You can't disagree there – anyway, so, I went to the bank, and I spoke English to him, OK? Now, so I impressed him. I – beaten him at – at – he didn't know – he didn't know much language, so he was stopping every two minutes to think about it – right? – and I pretended I didn't know more Punjabi, so I was forcing him to speak English.

Say the Word (Bretton Hall College 1977)

Another kind of English that nowadays has a strong influence in the world is American English. Since the end of the second world war, America has become the world's top industrial power and it dominates a large part of the world, through trade, entertainment, telecommunications, and political alliances. With all this power, the influence of American English has been immense. American magazines, TV and pop music have exported the language of Kojak and Coca Cola across the globe. It affects the way all of us speak and write English in Britain by introducing new words and styles.

Here are some examples of American English

I realise that, for many Britons (and not just for certain over-60s), the notion that Americans have donated any valuable words or expressions to us is painful. Yet how much poorer English would be without expressions like 'barking up the wrong tree', 'take it easy', 'I should worry', 'making a song and dance'. How could we dispense with words like 'boss', 'stampede', 'streamlined', 'highfalutin' and 'gobbledygook'? Would the English purist deprive himself of 'transistors', 'detergents', 'telephones' and 'cornflakes'? What native substitutes would he offer for expressions like 'to soft-pedal', 'lame duck', 'ballyhoo', 'backlash', 'brainwash' and 'striptease'?

Not so harmless is the pompous jargon which American sociologists and government spokesmen have devised in recent years. NBC's senior commentator, Edwin Newman, is running a one-man crusade against defilers of the language.

'I received a letter from a reader not long ago – and I've received hundreds upon hundreds of them – about a sociologist (they're the worst offenders) at the University of Southern California who, in describing murder and assault, classified them as "escalated interpersonal altercations". Now, if you believe that you're contributing to understanding or learning by calling murder and assault, anything but murder and assault, obviously you're misleading people. It's a very bad idea not to refer to murder and assault as precisely what they are . . . May I give you another example? The Atomic Energy Commission of the United States put out a press release about an experiment with fish in which all the fish had died, but the agency would not say that all the fish had died. It said the "biota exhibited 100 per cent mortality response" . . . And, of course, Vietnam was the great source of that kind of thing. "Bombing, bombing, why do you always say bombing?" one of the military spokesmen was quoted as saying. "These are protective reaction strikes." '

Very American, Very Stiff Upper Lip TONY CASH (*The Listener* 15 January 1976)

1 Look back to the description of Turkish migrant workers arriving in Germany. Notice the kinds of things that the newcomers found strange. Then try to recall an occasion when you visited another country or another part of Britain. Write an account of what you heard and saw on arrival, and try to describe your feelings.

2 Collect examples of American English words and expressions to fit into a table like this. Try to find ten examples for each column.

Food	Music	Fashion	Entertainment	Others
Hamburger	cool	Levi's	movies	hang-up

3 Choose one area of life you've mentioned in Question 2 above. Then write a few sentences about how the United States has influenced that area. Use the words you have collected as evidence for your ideas.

4 Using pictures from a magazine, or by drawing your own, make up an advert for English English. (Think of a suitable caption such as 'English English –The Original'.) Or do the same for any other kind of English you know – Cockney, Geordie, Jamaican English, etc.

Social groups and standard English

In the next few pages we are going to look at how social status and power affect the way people speak English – and also at the ways in which criticisms are made of the language of those people without much status or power.

First of all, we need to look at how our society is organised. One common way of doing this is to divide people up into three groups – upper, middle and lower. You can more or less tell which group people belong to by their accent.

The upper group possess money, property, power and control over the way the country is run. They include landowners, directors of large companies, the Royal Family and other aristocracy, the government, leaders of the armed forces, universities, mass media, etc. They have mostly attended Public Schools.

The lower group are manual workers, in factories, docks, farms etc. Although this is the largest of the three groups, individuals in it do not have the money or the power to influence others much. For this reason, manual workers united to form trades unions.

The middle group are difficult to describe. Some are close to the upper group because they have sizeable amounts of money and property (eg owners of small factories) or because they hobnob with them (eg rich pop stars, TV presenters). But at the other end of this group are people whose background and lives are closer to manual workers (eg secretarial and office workers).

The upper group and some of the middle group are able to spread the idea that their ways of speaking English – their accents and their dialect – are best. Schools often say that the only correct way to speak is in standard English dialect and with received pronunciation – that is, like a TV newsreader.

Standard English is

- using the words you find in a dictionary
- putting those words together in the ways that a TV newsreader or a posh newspaper does, using their grammar
- not using a local dialect, words or phrases – for example not using *ain't* (but *have not, are not,* etc.) *we was* (but *we were*) *I didn't do nothing* (but *I didn't do anything*)
- at its most standard when it comes to spelling and punctuation
- found in most writing, including the commentary in this book
- something that varies in different English speaking countries
- nothing to do with people's accent and pronunciation

Received Pronunciation is

- pronouncing words like a TV newsreader or an Oxford professor
- something that varies even among those people
- not using a local accent
- not speaking ultra posh, 'frafly frafly'.

Standard English is sometimes called by other names:

    a. The Queen's English
    b. BBC English
    c. Educated English

a. The Queen's English

"Why didn't you get the job?"

"They said I didn't speak the Queen's English."

The Queen speaks standard English dialect, though not with received pronunciation. She often includes such standard phrases as 'my husband and I' (as opposed to 'me and my husband') in her Christmas speeches.

b. BBC English

The BBC certainly has a lot to do with deciding what counts as standard English and then spreading it throughout Britain. There used to be a BBC committee which decided what words should be spoken on TV and radio and how they should be pronounced. The committee were mainly university professors, famous authors and others representing the upper group. Here is an account of one of their problems: how should you say 'margarine'?

After some hesitation, the committee voted for *marjarine*, defying the makers, who did not care for the soft 'g' presumably because the hard 'g' was thought to be used by more genteel folk, and the companies wanted marge to be linked with gracious living. A letter was sent to the *Daily Herald* from the secretary to the Margarine Manufacturers' Association:

'The word is derived from the Greek word, *margaron*, meaning a pearl, and, during the 60 years in which margarine has been in use in this country, it has always been given the hard 'g' by the manufacturers and distributors. If the BBC pronunciation is to be accepted, then the name Margaret, which is also derived from *margaron*, will have to be pronounced *Marjaret*.'

This letter was reported to the BBC committee. After discussion, the committee decided that, in view of the fact that the word *marjarine* was commonly used both by those who bought and those who sold the product, there was not sufficient justification for reversing their previous recommendation.

English as She is Spoke PAUL FERRIS (The Listener 22 December 1977)

How often do you hear the six o'clock news read by someone with a Glasgow accent?

This is thi
six a clock
news thi
man said n
thi reason
a talk wia
BBC accent
iz coz yi
widny wahnt
me ti talk
aboot thi
trooth wia
voice lik
wanna yoo
scruff. if
a toktaboot
thi trooth
lik wanna yoo
scruff. yi
widny thingk
it wuz troo.
jist wanna yoo
scruff tokn.
thirza right
way ti spell
ana right way
ti tok it. this
is me tokn yir
right way a
spellin. this
is ma trooth.
yooz doant no
thi trooth
yirseltz cawz
yi canny talk
right. this is
thi six a clock
nyooz. belt up.

TOM LEONARD from
Three Glasgow Writers
(Molendinar Press)

12

c. Educated English

Standard English is sometimes confused with speaking in a posh accent – an Oxford accent or a public school accent. But you can talk standard English in any accent, as a lot of educated people do on TV and radio every day.

Both standard English and posh accents are used in our society as ways of judging people, as if those who don't speak like that would really like to but can't manage it.

1 Keep a record of the different accents you hear on TV in one evening – who was speaking, about what, in what accent, on what programme.

Name of TV programme	Who was speaking	What accent	What about	What did you think of it

2 Look back at the poem about newsreaders by Tom Leonard. Try writing (and tape recording) your own version of a topical news item and then either read it in your own accent or in any other accent that you can imitate.

3 Do you think there is such a thing as proper English? Can you describe it? Who speaks it?

4 Write a conversation, trying to bring out the accents and dialects between any two of the people on p.9.

Change in group, change in language

A lot of worrying about *how* people speak takes our minds off *what* they're saying, yet it's *what* people say that should really be seen as the important thing. 'Is it daft twaddle?' should be a more important question than 'Does he say his 't's' nicely?'

If you change your spoken language a lot as you get older, you may be cutting yourself off from your own relations and friends to join a new social group. It could mean that you are cutting yourself off from your roots.

In order to belong to the middle group, some people have changed their accents deliberately, to 'get on' in the world. Here some school pupils whose parents work in manual jobs describe what happened when they went to grammar schools.

Speech and accent had been an early difficulty. Some spoke of their sudden self-consciousness over accent, of their discovering that they actually had an accent. Boys were troubled at having to read aloud in class, girls feared to ask questions. 'That bothered me quite a lot. I thought that if I mispronounced words or said them wrongly the other girls would pick me up and correct me and tease me . . . Oh yes, they did. Oh yes, they certainly did. These things did happen.' But, as confidence gathered, some of these troubles were deliberately overcome. Parents with middle-class ambitions were as conscious over this particular difficulty as their children, and a small number (especially girls) were soon taking elocution lessons. Others spoke of themselves as good 'mimics' who quickly learned to speak as others and the teachers spoke. This group, 'the mimics', were perhaps the largest body, and they certainly knew what they were about. 'Fairly early on I decided what changes I was going to make in my accent and I made them. That's perhaps why there was that drifting apart that I told you of from all the other children.' So shifts in accent too play their part in loosening 'neighbourhood' ties, and it was as if the process continually gathered momentum and the breach grew wider. But accent, even if changed, was still a burden and created other difficulties. That it offended the neighbours and old friends goes almost without saying (stuck up, speaks la-di-dah), but this time it cut into the home and family life. Again the need was above all for 'tact', and there were children who became bilingual, speaking BBC English at school but roughening up when they got home. But the situation was not as automatic as this, and the tact was not always forthcoming. Some kept the new accent at home as well as at school, and though this was approved by parents paying for elocution lessons, it thrust a touch of discord into other working-class homes.

Education and the Working Class B. JACKSON and D. MARSDEN (Penguin)

If you refuse to change your accent and to drop a few non-standard English phrases it can cause difficulty if you are trying for certain middle-group jobs. These phrases might be something as tiny as saying 'ain't', 'we was' or 'I don't do no Science' (standard English: 'isn't', 'we were', 'I don't do any Science'). Here is an example:

Dear Mr Stevens,
You may not recognise the name but I was chairman of the panel which interviewed you on 28 March for the vacancy as Lecturer Grade 1 in Sociology at Woolwich College for Further Education when no one was appointed.

I am writing to give you some personal advice which I hope you will accept in the spirit it is given, to help a young man whom most of us felt had much to offer if one failing could be eradicated.

We were generally impressed by your written statement and you interviewed well except that we were all very worried by grammatical and other faults in your spoken English. It is not a question of accent but of grammar and aspirates, (dropped h's) looseness of which could we felt be harmful for pupils and inhibit full cooperation with colleagues, this being a college where there is full harmony. I hope that on reflection you will appreciate this viewpoint and take steps to remedy the failing as we feel this would greatly assist your future in the profession.
Yours sincerely,
K. F. Valpy

Language and Class (Language and Class Workshop)

There is still a lot of prejudice in Britain about the accents and dialects of working people. We need to remember that an attitude to language is never *just* an attitude to language. It's also a judgment about the people involved. If I criticise the way you talk, I am criticising you.

1 With a partner, make up an imaginary conversation between the driver of a Rolls Royce and the driver of a lorry which has just crashed into it.

2 Try to remember a time when someone commented on your speech, to praise it or to criticise it or to get you to speak 'nicely'. Write down all the times you can remember when this has happened to you and your friends. Do you think that the change suggested would have made any difference to the ideas you were trying to put across?

3 With a partner, try to work out which of the following things you can tell about a person just by hearing their voice: education, intelligence, looks, social group, sex, age, birthplace, height, personality, physical strength, income?

Local dialects and accents

One of the great things about English and other languages is the number of different accents and different dialects in which they are spoken. Here are a few examples. Your teacher will probably be able to show you more and the people in your class will know a lot between them.

Living in the North East of England, as I have been for the last two years, is a bit like being in a foreign country: they say things differently there. I am a Londoner, accustomed to calling a sparrow by its proper name, but in Newcastle-on-Tyne this bird is a 'spuggy'. London sparrows often look dirty, and their Geordie cousins aren't noticeably cleaner: hacky mucky spuggies are a common sight. In the south, children eat sweets, or sweeties, but on Tyneside it's bullets they devour. An apt word, it occurs to me, for those deadly little objects which ensure that the toothy of today will be the dentured of tomorrow. Newcastle children, visiting the seaside, don't paddle, they plodge; a nice word, that, suggestive of mud and messiness. I realise now that when, as a boy, I went to Southend I didn't paddle, I plodged.

In Newcastle, familiar words take on different meanings. Dad, for example, is a verb meaning to beat or to beat a mat; bait is a packed meal, and when people bubble they cry. If a southerner describes a person as canny, he is indicating that he or she is cautious, even cunning, but in the North East the word signifies approval: a canny man is someone to be respected.

from *Sprechen Sie Geordie* PAUL BAILEY (*Words* BBC)

Biby's' Epitaph

A muvver was barfin' 'er biby one night,
The youngest of ten and a tiny young mite,
The muvver was poor and the biby was thin,
Only a skelington covered in skin;
The muvver turned rahnd for the soap off the rack,
She was but a moment, but when she turned back,
The biby was gorn; and in anguish she cried,
'Oh, where is my biby?' — The angels replied:

'Your biby 'as fell dahn the plug-'ole,
Your biby 'as gorn dahn the plug;
The poor little thing was so skinny and thin
'E oughter been barfed in a jug;
Your biby is perfeckly 'appy,
'E won't need a barf any more,
Your biby 'as fell dahn the plug 'ole
Not lorst, but gorn before.

(London)

A farmer sent his son to the agricultural college, and so he sent him there, and when he came back his uncle was passing one day and thought he'd call in and see how he was getting along. Well, the old farmer says, 'Oh, he farms t'same, tha' knooaws, but he talks so different,' he sez. 'Wherear he used to say "Whooa, Ned," to-t-horse, when it gait to t'end of t'furrow, an' "gee-up, lad", naow he sez "Halt, Edward" "Pivot", and proceed' He sez "Tha sees, t'horse doesn't know what he's talking abaht. So let mi' tell thi', lad, it's no good sending thi' lad to t'college, unless tha' sends t'horse, an' all.'

(Yorkshire)

Nowadays, fewer people speak local dialects. Many more people speak standard English (although they may speak it with a local accent). There are many reasons for this:
1 **the pressure of continually hearing standard English on radio and TV and in school,**
2 **the rise in office jobs,**
3 **the increased amount of moving about the country.**

Writing, with its standardised spelling and rules of punctuation, is a kind of standard English which is helpful for communicating with others, no matter how you or they speak.

This extract is from a story which takes place in Trinidad. The new English teacher encourages the class to talk in dialect but to write in standard English for the exams.

As he entered the classroom, I observed that he was a young man. His well-coiffured hair hung down to his shoulders. His penetrating, brown eyes focused on us; his voice was slightly metallic. But what fascinated us most about him was his manner of speech. It was to say the least unexpected!

He paced from one end of the room to the other.

'Ah name Ramoudit Singh; ah was born on de 30th December, 1950; ah come out from San Fernando. As all yuh know, ah come to teach English language, buh as all yuh will find out, ah believes in talking de language of de people. Dat way all yuh understan' mih, an' ah understan' all yuh. Right?'

He paused and looked at us intently.

'Ah know all yuh ain't too happy wid mih cutting in at dis present time, especially as dis is mih fust job, and wid English exam coming up just now, buh we go have to try to get along and see wha' we could do. Right?'

He resumed his pacing. He held the attention of the entire class. Eyes followed him from one place to another and back as he retraced a steady path. Utter silence from us students prevailed for that entire period. What was happening was unbelievable, but it was true.

'Ah ain't no bright man,' the new teacher continued, 'an' ah doh like people who feel dey hah too much in dey head. An nex' thing, doh feel all yuh inferior to mih, even doh ah hah mih GCE O Level, and all yuh ain't. We equal. De only ting is dat all yuh sitting down dey, an' I stannin' up here. Ah ain't really hah no more dan yuh, an' yuh ain't hah no more dan me. If yuh shy, ah doh believe we go get along, fuh in English we hah to convey ideas to each odder. An' we mus' convey dem in we mudder-tongue. Leave de fancy style fuh writin'.'

It was on his third day, however, that he surprised the class. He handed out Xerox copies of a passage for comprehension. In order to save time, oral questions and answers were to follow. The passage was one of the most beautifully-written bits of prose I had read for a long time.

'Is I self write dat wen ah was at school', Mr Ramoudit Singh claimed, 'an' now ah go ask all yuh questions to see if all yuh understan' it'.

I found it difficult to associate the passage with Mr Ramoudit Singh, and with the questions he began to ask in the 'mudder-tongue'. . .

Concerned as we all were about the possible results of our coming examinations, I was forced to wonder which posed the greater problem – translating 'English-as-written' into the 'mudder-tongue' for purposes of speech, or translating the 'mudder-tongue' into 'English-as-written' for exams and for communicating with the rest of the English speaking world?

The New Teacher, NINNIE SEEREERAM from *Backfire*
ed. U. and G. Guiseppe (Macmillan)

1 Write down your answers to these questions. Do you think you have a dialect? When do you use it? Do you enjoy using it? Are there times when you prefer using standard English? Are there things that you can say in dialect that you can't say in any other way? What sort of things? If you talk in dialect at home, how do your parents react? If you talk in dialect in class, how do your teachers react? Do you think that your dialect should be used in the classroom? In what way?

2 Look at the dialect maps on p.16. Then try to make your own list (or map) of different dialect words for playing truant or for stealing.

3 Write down a short conversation in standard English between two people at work. Then re-write it in as many different dialects as you can.

4 Have you ever had experiences similar to the man who wrote 'Sprechen Sie Geordie'? Describe a time when you were a stranger somewhere and had to get used to understanding the dialect of the local people; for instance, when you were on holiday.

5 Try reading (and perhaps recording) 'Biby's Epitaph' in a cockney accent, a posh accent, and any other accents you know. Write out 'Biby's Epitaph' in standard English.

6 Examine a piece of your writing which has been corrected by a teacher. Write down any mistakes which you think were made because you have written it in the way you speak. Try to explain each mistake.

7 Collect on tape examples of all the different accents, languages and dialects that people in your class know or use.

2 Language Rules

First kinds of talk

How can you talk about talk? How can you talk at all?

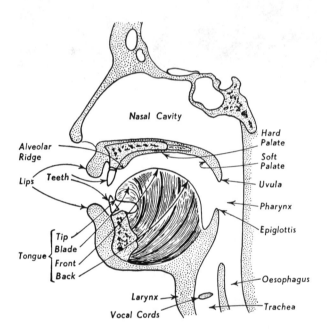

SONG: I keep on making noises

Well, I keep on making noises with my mouth
With my lungs and larynx, glottis, teeth and tongue
Don't ask me what I think it's all about
('cause I don't know)
I just open up my mouth and out it comes.

I make these noises every single day
And all my friends are making noises too
It's really quite addictive
And I hope that you won't laugh
When I tell you I make noises
By myself while in the bath
I make them while I'm working
I make them while at home
I sometimes even make them down the telephone
It's crazy. It's insane. It's quite beserk
But somehow it just seems to work
They call it talking
Somehow it just seems to work.

From the moment we are born, we start to make our needs known by a series of signs and sounds. Those who look after us learn to understand our cries and smiles. We learn to understand their smiles and sounds as we begin to grow.

In a doctor's waiting-room, a young father and mother had brought their very new baby. I saw the unsentimental shells of its ears, and its waving starfish fingers like something left stranded by the sea on a strange surrealist shore, an anemone in a pool. Then suddenly, as a shepherd hurriedly, shoutingly, pushes his flock through a gateway, the baby waved upwards, faster and faster, tempestuously flailing his arms with all his might – faster, faster – urgently shooing forth words towards the passionately working mouth that opened wide for a shout!

But the shout was soundless. Nothing. What was it the baby meant to say?

Babies are international. Lying in his cot, babbling as he grows, a baby speaks the consonants and vowels of every race in the world. . . .

Mmmm and *nnnn* he says, like a sexy woman, snuggling, desiring. And *ppp* and *ddd* he says, delighting in play. All over the world, mamans, mums, nanas and nannies, dads, pappas, pas and babushkas, we cry *'That's me!'* and turn his expressive sounds into the role we choose to play, answering him. This baby is amazed, and delighted. He makes his magic sounds again and again, and again we exclaim with joy and admiration, identifying ourselves as his family, and he crows in shared delight.

Still international, he continues to explore all the other sounds, he can make, joyously feeling out his abilities. But now he begins to notice when he has scored a bullseye. So he concentrates on the sounds these important adults like best, the ones they have chosen for their language, the ones they respond to; and he practises them. He has plenty of time to practise. None of this – neither the rich exploration, nor the mutual response, nor the selection, nor the concentration – has been taught him.

Look at Kids LEILA BERG (Penguin)

Between birth and the age of five years, children learn hundreds of words which describe their world. They learn to put them together in increasingly complex ways, though sometimes they don't use the right words at the right time.

As a child learns to speak it explores language; you also explore language, imitating the child as it makes efforts to imitate you. The process of learning becomes in itself a private language; you use baby talk which is only clear to your own child.

. . . But if you talk baby talk in the street people will think you're mad. . . . So you have to switch on different languages at different times. This is immensely confusing for the child. . . . It is a while before you can explain to a child why it is you encourage him to ask questions about everything at home, but if he asks a question about race or sex on the bus in a very loud voice, it is less easy to answer honestly, and more often than not you evade answering without explaining why.

Conditions of Illusion LEE CROMER

---

1 **Find out from your family if they can remember the first words you said.**

2 **Read the passage by Lee Cromer again. Write down some questions a child of five might ask that would be difficult to answer honestly on a crowded bus.**

3 **Choose only two of the babies on the next page. In what ways will they talk differently when they grow up? Accent? Dialect? Language? How do you know?**

22

Different kinds of talk

You can use language to

– express your wants and needs

> I want you to be my baby

– ask questions

> How's about we try?

– give commands

> Don't you ever leave me

– tell lies

> 'Cos if you do I'll die

– express complicated abstract ideas

> Love's a roulette wheel of emotion

– describe the past

> I've played a loser's game

– learn from the past

> But now I've learnt my lesson

– plan for the future

> I'm gonna try again

– make fantasies

> We'll live in a Wonderland
> Of rainbows and roses and wine

– understand your innermost thoughts and feelings

> Deep inside a little voice cries,
> 'We can make it, make it this time!'

– think about language itself

> Love's a word with many meanings;
> Maybe none of them are true –

– play with words

> But I'll wrap myself up in sticky tape
> To show I'm really stuck on you

– invent new words

> Wo-oh-wo-oh-wo-wo
> Shoo-be-do, oh yeah.

When it comes to talk, each one of us is an expert. We can speak and understand thousands of different kinds of talk without ever even noticing that we've got the skill. We even know how to change our talk, in fact change ourselves, to meet the demands of different situations.

Different people use different words to describe different situations.

The right way of saying something to one person may seem the wrong way to someone else.

I am an employer.	He's the boss.
She is an employee.	I'm a worker.
She is a packaging operative grade II.	I put things in boxes.
She is semi-skilled.	I'm bored stiff.
Each day she lunches in our on-site cafeteria.	Every day I have my dinner in the works canteen.
But we are currently rationalizing our man-power requirements.	They're giving us the sack.
She will then be entitled to unemployment benefits.	I can get the dole.
Pending such time as she secures further employment.	Till I get another job, if I get another job.

NOW, LET ME MAKE IT PERFECTLY CLEAR WHAT I MEAN WHEN I SAY MERRY CHRISTMAS...

1 Identify as closely as you can, the kind of speaker likely to have spoken these words. List them with their likely situations. The first one has been done for you.

Quotation	Speaker	Situation
Love fifteen	Umpire	Tennis match

Love fifteen
Once upon a time there was toad
Faced as we are with a grave economic crisis.
It's a fair cop guv.
Our Father
I wandered lonely as a cloud.
So the monk says to the commercial traveller . . .
Keep your kids off my begonias.
Banjo coupling from the fluid release valve.

2 **'Twas brillig, and the slithy toves**
   Did gyre and gimble in the wabe.
   All mimsy were the borogroves
   And the mome raths outgrabe.

   Write down as many reasons as you can to show that this poem is in English. For example, can you say all the words out loud? Can you think of other, real words that you could write in place of 'brillig' (or 'toves') to show that they belong to the same part of speech? Can you make up two more sentences, with the same pattern as these, by inserting common words in place of the unusual ones?

3 Try to write your own short poem including as many different functions of language as you can.

4 *I am an employer. He's the boss.* Write similar lists of sentences for a policeman and a teenager or a teacher and a pupil.

5 With a partner, work out how many different meanings you can give to this sentence, just by saying it in different ways:
   The Desperate Bicycles are top of the charts again this week.
   You should be able to get three or four fairly quickly; six is pretty good; ten or more, excellent.

Sharing meanings

Sharing a language and its meanings depends on us agreeing that when we speak together we all use roughly the same rules about what words mean and the way they can and can't be put together.

'Always the same table,' said the man, 'the same chairs, the bed, the picture. And the table I call table, the picture I call picture, the bed is called bed, and the chair is called chair. Why, come to think of it? The French call a bed "lee", a table "tahbl", call a picture "tahblow" and a chair "shaze", and they understand each other. And the Chinese understand each other too'.
'Why isn't the bed called picture?' thought the man, and smiled, then he laughed, laughed till the neighbours banged on the wall and shouted 'Quiet!'
'Now things are going to change,' he cried out, and from now on he called the bed 'picture'.
'I'm tired, I want to go to picture' he said, and often in the morning he would lie in picture for a long time, wondering what he would now call the chair, and he called the chair 'alarm clock'.

So he got up, dressed, sat down on his alarm clock and rested his arms on the table. But the table was no longer called table, it was now called carpet. So in the morning the man left his picture, got dressed, sat down at the carpet on the alarm clock and wondered what to call what.

He called the bed picture.
He called the table carpet.
He called the chair alarm clock.
He called the newspaper bed.
He called the mirror chair.
He called the alarm clock photograph album.
He called the wardrobe newspaper.
He called the carpet wardrobe.
He called the picture table.
And he called the photograph album mirror.

So:
In the morning the old man would lie in picture for a long time, at nine the photograph album rang, the man got up and stood on the wardrobe, so that his feet wouldn't feel cold, then he took his clothes out of the newspaper, dressed, looked into the chair on the wall, then sat down on the alarm clock at the carpet and turned the pages of the mirror until he found his mother's table.

The man thought this was fun, and he practised all day long and impressed the words on his memory. Now he gave everything new names: Now he was no longer a man, but a foot, and the foot was a morning and morning a man.

Now you can continue the story for yourselves. And then, like the man, you can change the other words round:
to ring is to stand,
to feel cold is to look,
to lie is to ring,
to get up is to feel cold,
to stand is to turn over the pages.

So we get this:
In the man the old foot would ring in picture for a long time, at nine the photograph album stood, the foot felt cold and turned over the pages on the wardrobe, so that his mornings would not look.

    A Table is a Table, PIETER BISHCEL (from *Story: the First Book,* Penguin)

A less joky example of a failure to agree on meanings was reported in the *Daily Mirror*, 4 April 1978. ▼

Baby dies in tragic mix-up

By ROGER TODD, Home Affairs Correspondent

BABY ■ ■ was battered to death – after a mix-up over words.

Social workers who might have saved him did not act quickly enough because they did not understand a warning message.

When ■ ■ parents moved to Cambridgeshire, the social services department there received a report from Suffolk.

Bruises

Officials in that county had been dealing with the family after bruises and lacerations were found on ■ ■ when he was three months old.

But a report said yesterday their message was misinterpreted in Cambridgeshire because the two departments did not use the same words.

Instead of being listed as a 'definite' victim of battering, ■ ■ was described only as 'suspected' victim.

As a result, the report said, the officials in Cambridgeshire did not have 'any sense of immediate urgency' about the case.

■ ■ died at seven months in December 1976 after being beaten by his parents. He had a fractured skull, ruptured liver and 13 broken ribs.

He also had extensive scald scars on his chest and thigh.

The judge – who said it was 'a crime that makes the blood run cold' – jailed his parents for eight years.

Vital

The report, which was commissioned by Suffolk and Cambridgeshire councils, said: 'There were unfortunate weaknesses of communication in this case.'

It said it was vital that local authorities used the same words to describe the danger in baby-battering cases.

These definitions and terms should be decided as quickly as possible.

1 Like the man in *A Table is a Table*, make up a new word for a common everyday object. It can be a real word or a nonsense word (like 'wug' or 'bipper'). Then get a partner to question you about it. See how long it is before he or she guesses what it's usually called.

2 All of us can use language so that we share meanings only with those we want to, so we can cut other people out. Rhyming slang is one example.

   i Write down some words and phrases in one of these special languages. Then write a translation of each in standard English.
   ii Try and translate this piece of backslang:
      Uddenlysay ehay artedstay anyay argumentyay ithway ishay eighbour-nay, ayayusingcyay imhay ofyay eadingtray onyay ishay oestay.

3 *Twenty Questions* is a good game for showing just how much we share meanings. Write down the name of a person, a place, or a thing. Then see if a partner (or the rest of the class) can guess what you have written down in less than twenty questions. The best players don't guess until they have narrowed down the answer by clever question-ing, eg alive (or dead)? in Britain (or abroad)? used in the home (or outside)?

Different meanings

It can come as a shock to discover that others do not share our meaning of a word.

I heard of a child who played all day inseparably with a boy called Johnny, a West Indian boy. Johnny's mother went to work and Mandy's didn't, so Johnny had his meals with Mandy and went home at night. When Mandy and Johnny were five they started school. Mandy came home — without Johnny.
'Where's Johnny, then?' said her mother.
A haughty shrug. Silence.
'Where is he?'
Silence.
'Is he coming later?'
Silence.
The mother, perplexed, left her and went inside to get tea ready. Then —
'Tea's ready. Has Johnny come?'
Silence.
'Isn't he having tea today?'
Silence.
'What's the matter? Where *is* Johnny? Have you had a quarrel? What's happened?'
'Well!' said Mandy, tossing her head with what Blake called Experience. 'He never told me he was black!'

Look at Kids LEILA BERG (Penguin)

'Black' is one of the most loaded words in the English language. People often use 'black' in phrases that mean:
. . . evil, as in *the black arts* and *black magic*; death, as in *the black death* and *the black flag*; disgrace, as in *black books, black marks, black list, black sheep, to black ball* and *to blacken*; and have criminal connotations, as in *blackmail* and *Black Maria*. Other associations, such as *black leg, blackguard* and *a black look* merely add to the negative picture which is filled out by such phrases as *the nigger in the wood-pile*.
All Things White and Beautiful BOB DIXON *in The Politics of Literacy*, ed M. HOYLES (Writers and Readers Co-op, 1977)

Immigrants

The chief change
I've noted
among
White Folks is
now they talkin
bout us in code.
Like,
Stateside when they
say:
crime in the streets or
welfare cheats
they talkin bout us.
An in Britain
when they say
Immigrants, guess
who they mean?
I mean, they got
Cypriots, Pakistanis,
Indians, Spanish an
Italians,
but, even if yo
Great-great-great-great
Grandaddy was the
Dude turned on Ol Will
in a stable an
caused him to write

Othello, you still
an Immigrant if yo
skin is other than
fish-belly white.
Quite!
Maybe it takes as
long to become
A Black Briton
as it does to grow
them Midlands lawns
nobody but birds
walk on.
That would be cool
if they laid the
same standards on
everybody else come
here since the
Norman Invasion.
Like,
how bout that
German Lady layin
up in Buckingham Palace?
I mean,
how come the Queen
ain't un
Immu-grunt?

Ammunition SAM GREENLEE (Bogle L'Ouverture)

But not everyone agrees that 'black' means something bad. For instance, the slogan 'Black is beautiful' tries to challenge the old meaning. A newer example of a loaded word is 'immigrant' which is often used to mean 'black people' although two out of three immigrants to Britain nowadays are white.

When we learn a language we take on a lot of the meanings that have been built into that language before we came along. For instance, the way we talk about men and women in English reveals attitudes towards men and women in our society.

Take the words *host* and *hostess.* A host is a man who entertains or gives shelter to a guest or visitor. A hostess, though commonly used to describe a woman entertaining at home, can also be a polite way of saying *prostitute.* . . .

Similarly, when you call a man a *tramp,* even though that is not particularly flattering, you are describing his way of life. But to call a woman a *tramp* is to condemn her sexual morals.

When you call a man *an honest man* you mean that his honesty and integrity can't be questioned. But when you refer to a woman *as an honest woman,* you are referring to her sexuality, implying that she is sexually pure or faithful. . . .

. . . the word *landlord* has the ring of ownership and possessions, while *landlady* is not quite so grand. She is more of a housekeeper who imposes petty restrictions.

Compare how the words *king* and *queen* are used. *King* is the more powerful word. In advertising it is used to suggest size – something big, the best you can get. So you sell an expensive brand of cigarettes by calling them *king-sized.* Size is only another indication of power. This is not so when the word *queen* is used. Usually it is applied to what is basically trivial. There are *May queens, beauty queens, Post Office Machinery queens.* And if the word is not used trivially it is used in a rather offensive way about a homosexual man.

The word *man* itself is used to convey the idea of power and size. *Man-sized* tissues are larger and stronger than *feminine* tissues, which are pastel-coloured, perfumed and fragile. We hear the words *man*power, chair*man*, sports*man*ship used often when it is women we are talking about. How many more can you think of. . . .?

The idea that women are passive creatures is reflected in the language we use about them when we are being complimentary as well as abusive. The words we use can identify women with plants and animals, but the most passive of them are connected with food. What can be more lifeless and passive than a plate of food? Women are:
> *honey*
> *sugar*
> *cheesecake*
> *sweetie pies*

They have *cherry lips* and *peaches-and-cream* complexions. They look *delicious,* like *delectable morsels,* they look *good enough to eat.* Even as a compliment, the food they are compared with is different, delightful perhaps, but somehow frivolous, whereas men are described as *beefcake,* or *hunks of meat* – much more substantial. The superiority of men over women is reflected in the grammar of our language. A good example of this is the way in which the personal pronoun is used. *He* is used, not only to mean *he,* but also to mean *he* and/or *she.* This applies even when there is only a theoretical possibility that there is a man present. It may sound strange to an audience that is largely women to be referred to as *he* but this is what usually happens. If you said *she*, any male present would feel immediately excluded. . . .

We've looked at how words themselves are used. There are also differences in the actual speech of men and women. . . .

I find my husband has two separate vocabularies. If I talk to the woman next door I'm *gossiping*, but if he talks to her husband he's *discussing things;* if I close my eyes while sitting in the easy chair, I'm *dozing off;* when he does the same thing he's *contemplating;* when I'm silent I'm *moody*, whereas he, of course, is *being thoughtful.*

> letter in a women's magazine *The Gender Trap — Book 3*
>
> *Messages and Images —* C. ADAMS *and* R. LAURIKIETIS (Virago 1976).

1 **Make as long a list as you can of words which we have borrowed from other languages.**
   Dictionaries often tell you the origins of words in brackets at the end of the definition eg F for French in 'café – coffee house, restaurant (F-coffee)'.

2 **Make a list of all the jobs you can think of under the three headings female, male and neutral. Compare your list with a partner and work out why some jobs have different names according to which sex is employed. Make up new neutral names which can apply equally to men or women.**

Female	Male	Neutral
Actress	Actor	Player
Nurse	Male nurse	
Authoress	Author	

3 **Choose a news story from a newspaper. Underline or copy out any words or phrases which you think have different meanings for different people. Compare your answers with your friends.**

Changing meanings

Words can change their meaning for many reasons, as a glance at any good dictionary will show.

Science and technology are probably the most prolific providers of new words today. The exploration of the moon has given us words for novel experiences: *moonwalk, earthrise* . . . exploration of deep space provides us with: *quasars, pulsars, neutron stars* and the mysterious *black hole.*

Medicine too is a major contributor of new terms such as . . . *busulfan, open heart surgery* and the *pill.* But science and technology are not the only sources of new words. A decade and a half since the publication of Webster's International Dictionary has seen considerable political and social ferment which has left its mark on the language. . . .

Young people have spurned the establishment to join the *counter culture* as *hippies* or *flower people* or *punks*. Their music has given us *acid rock, hard rock* cheered loudly by *teenyboppers* and *groupies*. English gets its vocabulary from many new fields but these new words are for the most part, created or derived in a number of time honoured ways. Not all new words are in fact new. Old words are frequently given new meanings to fit new situations. *Angel,* for example, is the meaning given to a spiritual being believed by many to be able to exert an influence on men without them being aware of his presence. Now the word *angel* is also used for a radar echo whose cause is not visually discernible. The dove is a traditional symbol of peace and the hawk is a predatory bird, so *dove* has come to be used for a conciliatory person, *hawk* for one who is militant.

A Supplement to Webster's Third International Dictionary,
(G. & C. Merriam Co, Springfield, Mass, USA.)

Sometimes the words do not exist for what we want to say so we have to change the rules.

Recently, I agreed to take on the responsibilities of what is customarily known as a godmother to the son of a friend of mine when he was christened. As an agnostic (someone who does not believe in God) I felt awkward with such a title and so decided to invent a new name for my new position: alt-mother, meaning alternative mother. So now my alt-son has three godparents and one alt-mother to keep an eye on him as he grows up.

MARGARET SANDRA (*Feminist Research Group,* 1978)

Here are a riddle, a poem and a proposal, all challenging our assumptions about words and their meanings. Can you work out the meanings?

The blind beggar's brother died. The
brother who died had no brother. What
relation was the blind beggar to the blind
beggar's brother?

Awareness

BLACK	PEOPLE	THINK
PEOPLE	BLACK	PEOPLE
THINK	PEOPLE	THINK
BLACK	PEOPLE	THINK
THINK	BLACK.	

Mixed Bag DON LEE (Scott, Foresman & Co. 1970)

Searching the roots of Western civilisation for a word to call this new species of men and women, someone might come up with 'gen' as in 'genesis' and 'generic'. With such a word, 'man' could be used exclusively for males as 'woman' is used for females, for 'gen' would include both sexes. Like the words 'deer' and 'bison', 'gen' would be both plural and singular. 'Gen' would express the warmth and generalised sexuality of generous, gentle and genuine: the specific sexuality of genital and genetic. In the new family of 'gen', girls and boys would grow to 'genhood' and to speak of 'genkind' would be to include all the people of the earth.

Is Language Sexist? from *Men and Women Work with Language,*
S. HARRIS and K. MORGAN (E. J. Arnold)

1 Collect a list of 20 words which did not exist 50 years ago, or which are used in a new sense now, eg cheeseburger, Babylon, disco, jeans, chauvinist, comprehensive. Then write out a short explanation of why each new word (or meaning) has developed.

2 Make up names for
  i. a new pop group;
 ii. a drug to stop people smoking;
iii. a very strong glue.
   Give reasons as to why you think your names are good ones. What impression do they create?

Remember – language rules but only if you let it!

3 Says Who?

Different situation, different kind of talk

We all know that we talk in different ways in different places at different times with different people about different things. It all depends on the situation we are in. That's what this part is all about. But it's worth remembering, for a start, that there are some places that most people can't get into anyway. So most of us don't get a chance to talk there at all, even though the people who *do* get in may affect our lives a lot.

In a lot of situations, there are definite limits on *who* does the talking and *who* stays silent.

Silence in court!
No talking in the ranks.
If you want to say something, put your hand up, Jones.
Let's talk about your back-pay later shall we Jones?
Don't talk with your mouth full, Derek.
Ssh!
Shut up!

There are also limits on *what* you're supposed to talk about and *the way* you're supposed to talk about it. Here are two cases where something went wrong – or was it right? The first one is supposed to have happened some years ago. Can you think of a similar modern example?

A poor girl from the East End of London was invited to a charity tea at the home of a local magistrate's wife.

The little girl sat down at the table, turned to her fine hostess and said:

'I see you keep your house very clean. Cleanliness is next to godliness, you know.'

The lady smiled, and gave her husband a knowing look.

'Is your husband working?' asked the little girl.

'But of course!' said the lady. 'What a strange question for you to ask.'

'And are you both keeping off the drink?'

'What an impertinent little girl!' cried the magistrate's wife. 'When you are out visiting you should take care to behave like a lady, my child.'

'But I do!' said the little girl. 'When the ladies visit our house, they always ask those questions!'

Big Red Joke Book (Pluto Press 1976)

Ginger Evans winked at somebody and then looked again at me, his voice all friendliness, his eyes brilliant with mischief.

'Thought you might have been used to calling teachers "sir",' he said, 'You don't do that with Charlie. He's one of these modern teachers. You call him "Charles" and you stick "Charles" on to everything you say if you don't want him to belt you. "Yes, Charles." That's how you do it. "Thanks very much, Charles." Got it? You do that and you'll be OK. That right, you lot?'

They were nodding and grinning, and one or two of them were near to bursting.

'You must think everybody's as daft as you are, Evans,' the big boy said.

Ginger didn't hear him. He was too anxious to fill me with information.

'Charlie's got a stick, kid. Keeps it in that cupboard. Most of the teachers don't cane you but Charlie does and Timber Thompson sometimes. Gutsy Collins – he takes PT – he uses a slipper. But Charlie's the one to watch. If he uses his stick on you it feels like you've been guillotined. So you give him five bob for your dinners so's he can spend it on whisky at night and you call him "Charles" and you'll be OK. That's how we do it. Isn't that right, you lot?'

There were frenzied nods and giggles which were strangled when Mr Harris walked into the room. He looked at me.

'You're the new boy. Stewart, is it?'

'Yes, Charles,' I said.

There was a network of tiny purple veins over his cheeks and these were suddenly lost in the redness that flushed into his face. His bottom lip was slightly trembling.

'Somebody told you to say that,' he said and the trembling of his lip became a trembling of his voice. 'Somebody told you to address me in that way. Who was it, Stewart?'

I nodded at Ginger. 'This boy told me your name.'

'When you address me, Stewart,' Mr Harris said, 'call me "sir". "*Sir*", boy.' He went to the cupboard beside the blackboard and without looking at the class he said, 'Come out, Evans!'

Ginger came out, his face brighter than his hair. As he walked past me he punched me in the stomach so hard that I gasped.

'*Snitch*' I heard somebody whisper.

The boys were glaring at me; all except the big boy next to Ginger. He was smiling a little as he watched me, a shy embarrassed smile.

Mr Harris was holding his cane. It was about three feet long and half an inch thick and it had the cruel curve of a scimitar.

'Your hand, Evans', he said. 'This is for impertinence.'

Dragon in the Garden REGINALD MADDOX (Macmillan Topliner)

1 Often the 'rules' for talking and not talking are not written down. They are taken for granted. Write out three hidden rules which affect the way you talk in each of these situations
   − with your friends in the playground
   − at mealtime at home
   − in a certain lesson.

2 Write down for a new pupil, in the first year or from another country, the rules for talking/not talking in your school.

3 You've seen a fight (or an accident) in the street near where you live. Write down how you would describe it to (a) a close friend (b) a policeman (c) an adult who you know well.

4 'Who says I should behave like that?'
   Choose a popular teenage magazine, and examine it carefully.
   What impression does the magazine try to give of
   i. the perfect teenager
   ii. the perfect life for a teenager?
   Make a list of all the ingredients you can find.

Power talks

The more power we have in a situation, the more we can dominate the conversation. Top people have most power in most situations they are in. Here are three examples of just such domination, taken from three different institutions.

School

I don't care whether you understand it or not, just get on with it.

Television

And to sum up . . . (thinks: I like this game − I always win!)

Church

No slave owner allowed his slaves to attend church by themselves, fearing that they would use the opportunity to plan an insurrection rather than thank God that they had such 'good' masters. So, the slave owner either did the preaching himself or hired a white preacher, or let a trusted slave preach. The only preaching a slave owner approved of was that which would make the slave happy to be a slave.

To Be a Slave JULIUS LESTER (Penguin)

The less power we have, the less confident with language we are likely to be. Our role isn't fixed, though. It can change from moment to moment, if we meet a different person or talk about something different. A person with more power in one situation may have less power in another.

So people have different faces to fit different places and sometimes people change so much from one place to another, from one situation to another, that it can be hard to tell which one is the real person talking, which one is the real you? In a way they *all* are.

SONG: Jim's the kid

Jim's the kid the teachers hate when he's at school
But Jim's the apple of his father's eye
And Jim's mates call him hard nut, tough guy, Mr Cool
But Jim's girl Julie thinks he's sweet as pie.

Julie's boyfriend Jim calls Julie soft sweet names
But Julie's friends say Julie's hard as nails
Her teachers think she's energetic, good at games
But her parents say she's lifeless tired and pale.

No one quite agrees about Jim and Julie
It makes no sense – just can't explain
Everybody sees a different picture
And the name's the only thing that stays the same.

---

1 See how easy or difficult it is to switch roles in school.
   i. Try becoming the teacher (in turn) while the teacher becomes one of the class.
   ii. Imagine that the classroom is the school hall. In turns, take an assembly.
   Then discuss how convincing you all were.

2 Write a story about an occasion when somebody felt unable to speak very much. It may be that they were being browbeaten or were somewhere for the first time or felt angry or lost or in love.

3 Re-read the song *Jim's the kid*. Write down a list of people who know. After each name write down what they call you (eg Jim, Smith, Son, Mr Smith, etc) and how you feel about it.

Getting your own way

There are a lot of different ways in which people try to show their superiority through language. The most obvious method people use is by giving orders – simple, blunt commands. They really do show who is boss. But only people who are really sure of their power and who are confident about throwing their weight around use orders to get their way. It seems less crude, more polite, to ask questions, for instance — even if the result is the same.

'Where's your light?' he snapped at Michael.
'It's broken, it's at home,' answered Michael.
'That's no excuse,' growled the policeman, 'you should always have a front light.' He looked at the boys and then at the bicycles.
'What make is your bike?' he asked Michael. 'What colour is it?'
Michael looked down at the bicycle.
'Don't look down,' snapped the policeman.
'It's red,' came the answer. The policeman passed onto Geoff.
'What make is your bike?' he asked.
'Tarmaster,' answered Geoff.
'What colour are your mudguards?' Geoff looked at the mudguards, then at the policeman.
'Red,' he answered.
'What make are your brakes? And don't look down this time.' Geoff looked down.
'Look bonehead,' shouted the policeman, 'I told you not to look down.'

The Gates, BILLY HOUSE and LESLIE MILDENER (Centerprise 1975)

But there are other ways of persuading people to do what you want, apart from giving commands and asking questions. In some institutions, a simple statement may get the job done if you're one of the top people. The point is that you can't tell if an order is really just an order, a question really just a question, or a statement just a statement, unless you know a lot about the situation and the people involved.

I'm a reasonable man
It will be your time you'll be wasting
after school.
I'll treat you like babies if you act the fool.
Whatever happens I get paid anyway.
Until you grow up I can sit here all day.
You'll be the one doing the exam, not me,
Your parents pay the rates, it doesn't
come free.
If you don't stop now I shall get cross.
I can take a joke, but that one's a dead loss.
I see the rest of the form think it's great fun,
So you can go to your housemaster and
say what you've done.
Maybe he will put you on report.
You're fifteen and your time here is short.

SIMON CROFT

There are other ways of showing who is who. One way is by talking down to people. Another is by using jargon words that nobody else can understand. Here are two examples – the second has been translated for you.

In the technotronic society the trend would seem to be towards the aggregation of the individual support of millions of uncoordinated citizens, easily within the reach of magnetic and attractive personalities effectively exploiting the latest communication techniques to manipulate emotions and control reason.

ZBIGNIEW BRZEZINSKI (National Security Advisor to Jimmy Carter, President of the United States of America)

Or, to put it another way:
In our kind of society, full of machines and electronics, the trend would seem to be towards using attractive personalities in TV, radio and newspapers to control the minds and feelings of millions of individual citizens.

Or, if you still haven't switched off:
If you control the media you can fool all the people all of the time.

If words fail us we can call on force or violence to try to make sure that our rules for language are observed – especially if we've got the power.

All in all, there are lots of ways in which some people get more say than others and in the following extract, the poor old hero gets put down in a lot of different ways by the two women. See how many you can spot.

Never in my life had I been in a bar of any sort. I knew from the films that you used various phrases to ask people what they would like to drink, and with a small satisfaction I remembered one from a picture we had seen at Dickie's the previous Saturday. 'What's your poison?' I said, moving close to her and looking into her dark Surbiton eyes. She giggled disconcertingly and said firmly: 'Gin and ton for me'.
I went to jelly. Gin and ton! Whatever it was, it sounded as though it cost quids. I would have to tell her, I just would, there was no going on with this.

But she smiled like sunshine before I could confess and she said: 'We'd better hurry, darling.'

Darling! This angel, with her high-heeled shoes and her gin and ton, had called me darling! Me with my yellow tie and my suit . . .

The endearment caught me up in a cloud and I staggered towards the bar. She was in love with me then. Girls didn't call you darling unless they were in love with you. All the time she had been hiding it, and doing it very well too.

And she called me that – and other people were standing around and they must have heard her saying it too. When people were in love in films they said that, but I did not think she would call me it. Darling!

I wondered if the woman at the bar had heard her. 'Gin and ton please, darling', I said. 'Not so much lip', she replied smartly, and I realised what I had said. 'Gin and tonic is it, and what else?'

My feet, both of them, were on the ground again now. 'Nothing else, thanks', I whispered, 'I'm not drinking. How much is it?'

'You don't look old enough for a start', she said, pouring the gin anyway. 'That will be one and eight.'

I returned to the girl bearing the gin and tonic as though it were a love potion. 'Gin and ton', I said idly.

'Good', she sniffed. 'Aren't you going to have something?'

'I'm on the wagon', I said, feeling immediately pleased that the phrase tripped off so lithely. 'Football training, you know. We're not allowed to drink.'

'How boring', she said, pouring the remainder of my one and eightpence down her red throat. 'Let's get back to this awful concert. Really, when I came with Paul . . .'

This Time Next Week, LESLIE THOMAS (Corgi)

---

1 **With a partner try out the following conversations. Swop over parts after a while.**
   i. **Persuading mum/dad to give you £3.00 to buy an LP of a group they don't like.**
   ii. **A man in your house wants to watch a sloppy film on TV at the same time as a woman wants to watch football.**
   iii. **You want a party, so try to persuade a parent to stay out late.**

2 **Writing out what is *really* meant.**

Example	Real Meaning
Would you mind getting changed for PE?	Get changed now. You've got two minutes precisely. Or you're for it.

   Make up five or six further examples. They don't have to be from school, but can be taken from TV, radio, home, street, etc, as well.

3 **Read the Leslie Thomas piece again. Make a list of all the words and phrases that show a way of putting him down.**

4 **Write down a list of all the jargon words you can think of connected with**
   i. **Your favourite sport;**
   ii. **Your school.**

   They all have to be words that an outsider, who knew nothing about the sport or your school, would not understand.

Fitting in – or breaking the rules

Sometimes we leave a lot of things unsaid. We fit into the situation, such as when we're with friends or at school or at home, even when we don't agree with what is going on. Here is an example of somebody 'fitting in'. A boy's father is being interviewed about school open-day.

Father: The headmaster irritated me, I can't put me finger on it now . . . Aye, aye, he's talking to hisself, you know, wa'nt talking to me . . . he put my back up . . . and then there was this person, you know, family, father or something, instead of coming out, asking the teacher a question he knew what he'd gotta ask, he knew what answer he wanted to get, you see, I don't know how to explain it, like. I thought like, 'Mate you'm only asking that question, just to let people know you'm in the room', know what I mean, 'cos he wasn't listening to the bloke's answer, he'd already accepted whatever the bloke was going to say was right, you know what I mean, how can I explain that. I don't know how to put it . . . See now, I can't get up in a room and talk against teachers, like, I couldn't talk against you, because I'd be flabbergasted, I'd be 'umming and 'ahhing and I'd be worried stiff you know . . . I dunno how to say it, how to put it, 'cos I'd look around me and I'd think, 'These people don't want to know anyway' . . . If I could have been in a room with 'im (the head) you know on his own, without anybody hearing us, I could have said . . .

Interviewer: Could have said what?

Father: You're full of bull.

Learning to Labour PAUL WILLIS (Saxon House)

Sometimes we break the rules, to create humour, and get people to think again about something we take for granted – like lumberjacks are tough.

Lumberjack Song

1 I'm a lumberjack
And I'm O.K.
I sleep all night
And I work all day.

2 I cut down trees
I eat my lunch
I go to the lavatory
On Wednesday I go shopping
And have buttered scones for tea.

3 I cut down trees
I skip and jump
I like to press wild flowers
I put on women's clothing
And hang around in bars.

4 I cut down trees
I wear high heels
Suspenders and a bra
I wish I'd been a girlie
Just like my dear Pappa.

Chorus He cuts down trees
He wears high heels
(spoken rather than sung)
Suspenders . . . and a *bra*?
That's shocking, etc.
That's rude . . . tuttut . . . tuttut . . .

Monty Python's Big Red Book
(Eyre Methuen)

We can also change the rules of the game by asking new questions, and taking up a new position, and by saying what is usually unsaid. Here are two examples. In the first one, a rich gentleman farmer (Peter Weddenham) is talking to one of his old farmworkers (Sim Partridge) in Essex, sometime in the late 1940s.

A. 'Ded ye ever try to bring up a family o'five on ten shillin's a week, or less, Master?' Sim Partridge asked.

Mr Weddenham swallowed his indignation; it did not disagree with him so much as he expected.

'I never knew anything about these matters', he declared.

'You never wanted you should; you never made no enquirations anybody ever heard on', said the man coldly, 'you never cared how folk lived or died, so long as you got y'r work done. You had y'r hunting an' y'r shootin', an' y'r bellyful three times a day, dedn't ye?' His tone had changed in a strange fashion. It had ceased to be that of him who serves and was that of him who judges. Mr Weddenham's power of retort had gone.

'Really, my man', he began, but Sim Partridge shook his head.

'No', he said, 'no man o' your'n no longer. That bin over a long time. It was all a mistake. We worn't yourn, though you killed us if you thought you would, an' nobody would stop ye.'

'I never harmed any man in all my life', cried Mr Weddenham, deeply stirred. 'You misjudge me shamefully'. To be suffering this sort of talk was dreadfully wrong, but in vague fashion he knew that the old ploughman was talking to him on terms of an equality that he had admitted and must abide. 'I've never failed in my duty', he declared.

'Happen you thought you never done wrong', replied Sim Partridge, 'an happen you never thought about it at all. Why should ye ha' done? I ain't blamin' ye, I'm tellin' ye. You worn't brought up to think o' nobody but y'rself, you an' y'r father an' y'r gran'father. I know, being' I served all th' three o' ye. Many's th'time you an' yours bin an' showed y'r pretty cottages to y'r frien's, but you dussn't never ha' took 'em inside to see where th' rain come through the thetch, where th'owd rats an' sparrers an' starlin's bin flecked it, an' th'fire smoked an' there worn't nawthen on th' table 'cept bread an' taters.'

It was in vain that Peter Weddenham concentrated his thoughts on reply, that would not help. The ploughman was walking quietly away. Apparently he was satisfied; his mission fulfilled, he was leaving his old employer alone.

Right Forward Folk S. L. BENSUSAN (Routledge 1949)

B. In the hungry 'thirties the fabulously rich Lady Astor used to visit the slums of Glasgow and Edinburgh and lecture workers' families on the delights of cod-head soup. After one such lecture a fisherwoman stood up and said:

'That lecture was marvellous, your ladyship, but I have one question.'

'Go ahead by all means', Lady Astor replied.

'While we're eating the cod-head soup, who is eating the cod?'

Big Red Joke Book (Pluto Press 1976)

Or we can change the language rules and even get into those places that we're not supposed to, as Angela Davis and her sister did when they broke a ruling against their black skins in Birmingham, Alabama, USA, by using an unexpected kind of language.

Years later, when I was in my teens, I recalled this childish daydream and decided, in a way, to act it out. My sister Fania and I were walking downtown in Birmingham when I spontaneously proposed a plan to her: We would pretend to be foreigners and, speaking French to each other, we would walk into the shoe store on 19th Street and ask, with a thick accent, to see a pair of shoes. At the sight of two young Black women speaking a foreign language, the clerks in the store raced to help us. Their delight with the exotic was enough to completely, if temporarily, dispel their normal disdain for Black people.

Therefore, Fania and I were not led to the back of the store where the one Black clerk would normally have waited on us out of the field of vision of the 'respectable' white customers. We were invited to take seats in the very front of this Jim Crow shop. I pretended to know no English at all and Fania's broken English was extremely difficult to make out. The clerks strained to understand which shoes we wanted to try on.

Enthralled by the idea of talking to foreigners — even if they did happen to be Black — but frustrated about the communication failure, the clerks sent for the manager. The manager's posture was identical. With a giant smile he came in from his behind-the-scenes office saying, 'Now, what can I do for you pretty young ladies?' But before he let my sister describe the shoes we were looking for, he asked us about our background — where were we from, what were we doing in the States and what on earth had brought us to a place like Birmingham, Alabama? 'It's very seldom that we get to meet people like you, you know.' With my sister's less than elementary knowledge of English, it required a great effort for her to relate our improvised story. After repeated attempts, however, the manager finally understood that we came from Martinique and were in Birmingham as part of a tour of the United States.

Each time this man finally understood something, his eyes lit up, his mouth opened in a broad 'Oh!' He was utterly fascinated when she turned to me and translated his words.

43

The white people in the store were at first confused when they saw two Black people waiting in the 'whites only' section, but when they heard our accents and conversations in French, they too seemed to be pleased and excited by seeing Black people from so far away they could not possibly be a threat.

Eventually I signalled to Fania that it was time to wind up the game. We looked at him: his foolish face and obsequious grin one eye-blink away from the scorn he would have registered as automatically as a trained hamster had he known we were local residents. We burst out laughing. He started to laugh with us, hesitantly, the way people laugh when they suspect themselves to be the butt of the joke.
'Is something funny?' he whispered.
Suddenly I knew English, and told him that he was what was so funny. 'All Black people have to do is pretend they come from another country, and you treat us like dignitaries.'
My sister and I got up, still laughing, and left the store.

An Autobiography ANGELA DAVIS (Hutchinson)

---

1 Along the lines of the lumberjack song, try to make people think again. Write a short song which breaks a stereotype, eg a charlady, a bespectacled swot, a city gent at a football match.

2 Imagine you've left school and become a famous person. You're invited back to talk to the school speech day and you decide to say how it really felt – the problems as well as pleasures.

3 Describe a real incident when someone left a lot of things unsaid or when somebody said something that is usually not said.

4 Cut two people (or a picture with two people in it) out of a magazine. Cut some speech balloons and thought bubbles out of white paper and stick them onto the picture. Fill in the balloons and bubbles to show differences between what the people are saying and what they are leaving unsaid.

5 Is there something about your local area that you feel very strongly about – something wrong, for example, or something that could be improved, or some new feature that you'd like to see?

   Get together with one or two friends and write a letter to the editor of your local newspaper, putting your point of view.

4 True Stories

Stories all around

Everywhere we go, everywhere we look, there is material for stories. Everyone we hear, everything we read, every one of us, sooner or later gets round to telling a story. Every picture tells a story. Even our dreams, our daydreams and our night dreams, tell us stories. We can't get away from them.

As Roland Barthes says, 'Narrative is present in myth, legend, fable, tale, novella, epic, history, tragedy, drama, comedy, mime, painting, stained glass windows, cinema, comics, news items, conversation'.

Image-Music-Text R. BARTHES (Fontana)

a. The End

Professor Jones had been working on time theory for many years. 'And I have found the key equation', he told his daughter one day. 'Time is a field. This machine I have made can manipulate, even reverse, that field.'

Pushing a button as he spoke, he said, 'This should make time run backward run time make should this', said he, spoke he as button a pushing.

'Field that, reverse even, manipulate can made have I machine this. Field a is time.' Day one daughter his told he, 'Equation key the found have I and'. Years many for theory time on working been had Jones Professor.

END THE

b.

45

c. One year passed. My school days began, and I did not last very long. I used to go to school at Otting Street. They turned me down because of my nerves. I could not talk. I was at school for three months. At that time I had a baby sister, Gladys. When I left school I stopped at home, and every morning my Mum used to put me outside the front door. She used to ask me how many motors had passed and I used to answer by blinking my eyes. I blinked once for every motor that passed. My Mum understood this.

d. Now when I started in this business many years ago, I started in a circus. I started in Billy Smart's circus – Billy Smart – not the Billy Smart who is today – his father – 'cos I'm much older than Billy. And I remember his father said to me one day, he said, 'Maxie, would you like to be a lion tamer?' I said, 'I've no desire'. He said, 'There's money in it'. I said, 'What do I have to do?' He said, 'All you've got to do is walk in the lion's cage and put your head in its mouth'. I said, 'I should think so'. He said, 'Are you scared?' I said, 'I'm not scared – I'm just careful'. He said, 'I shouldn't be scared of that lion', he said, 'That lion's as tame as a kitten. He was brought up on milk'. I said, 'SO WAS I – BUT I EAT MEAT!'

e. When Houses Were Alive

One night a house suddenly rose up from the ground and went floating through the air. It was dark, and it is said that a swishing, rushing noise was heard as it flew through the air. The house had not yet reached the end of its road when the people inside begged it to stop. So the house stopped.

They had no blubber when they stopped. So they took soft, freshly drifted snow and put it in their lamps, and it burned.

They had come down at a village. A man came to their house and said: Look, they are burning snow in their lamps. Snow can burn.

But the moment these words were uttered, the lamps went out.

f.

GOING NUTS ON BOOZE

A crazed squirrel which chased children at Washingborough, Lincs, was thought to have rabies. But experts called in to examine him found he was drunk after waking early from hibernation and sampling something intoxicating.

You can probably guess where most of these stories came from, and the kind of person who made them. Here is a list, not in correct order, of authors and sources, which you can probably match up very quickly:

1. Anonymous journalist, *Daily Mirror*.
2. Inugpasugjuk, an Eskimo, in *Technicians of the Sacred* ed. J. Rothenburg. (Anchor Books).
3. Max Miller, *The Max Miller Blue Book. (Robson Books)*.
4. John Joseph Deacon *Tongue Tied,* (the autobiography of a man who cannot speak or even move his hands in a coordinated way).
5. William Blake, *Songs of Innocence and Experience*.
6. Frederic Brown *Nightmares and Geezenstacks* (NY Bantam).

Here's a very short story:
'The last man on earth decided to end it all. He climbed to the top of the Empire State Building and jumped. As he passed the 57th floor, he heard the phone ring.'

There are also stories that go on for ever. They usually involve repetition of some kind, like describing an army of ants moving a barn full of wheat, ant by ant, grain by grain, or they can go round and round for ever – like this one:

The Boy Who Dreamed

There was a boy who dreamed that he was in a beautiful garden. He walked through the garden until he came to a house with a thousand rooms. He opened the door and walked in. He walked through all the thousand rooms; in the last one he found a bed. He lay down and went to sleep. He dreamed that he was in a beautiful garden. He walked through the garden until he came to a house with a thousand rooms. He opened the door and walked in. He walked through all the thousand rooms; in the last one he found a bed. He lay down and went to sleep. He dreamed that he was in a beautiful garden. He walked through the garden . . .

(This is an endless story, if you tell it to your friends, you can go on and on and on with it, until they beg you to stop!)

Riddles and Rhymes and Rigmaroles, JOHN CUNLIFFE (Piccolo)

---

1 **See if you can think of some small incident – maybe something that happened to you, that would make a point, and make it into a very short story.**

2 **See if you can think of a story which would go on for ever, and then write out the first page of it.**

3 **People often tell stories about places they know well, to create an impression with people who don't know them.**

   What stories are told to primary school children in your area, to give them an idea of what is in store for them when they go to secondary school?

   Have you heard any stories about work places in your area?

   Do you know any stories of heroism or horror connected with local gangs or football matches or discos?

4 **Here's a famous and very boring news story:**
   'Small earthquake in Peru. Nobody hurt.'
   Try to write the most boring story in the world. Nothing exciting must happen, there must be no interesting characters, no heroic or villainous acts, no vivid descriptions. Make every word and every phrase as dull and turgid as possible.

Some features of all stories

Surprise, surprise. Every spoken or written story has a beginning, a middle and an end. Or does it? The French film-maker Jean-Luc Godard once said that all his films had a beginning, a middle, and an end – but not necessarily in that order!

The beginning tells us a lot about the story that is to follow. Usually, we tune in very quickly as a result of our past experience, so that we can predict a whole lot of things, such as:

   i. **the kind of story – fact/fiction, realism/fantasy,**
      Once upon a time.
  ii. **the genre – western, news item, science fiction, dirty joke, hospital romance, etc.**
      I said to the landlord of this pub – I said . . .
 iii. **what the story line will be about**
      He was an old man who fished alone and he had gone eighty-four days now without taking a fish.
 iv. **what kind of characters and setting there will be**
      I was not able to light on any map or work giving the exact locality of Castle Dracula.
  v. **storyteller's tone of voice – thoughtful, angry, matter of fact, nudge nudge say no more, etc.**
      It was reported yesterday.
 vi. **the kind of language (style) the author will use – down-to-earth, literary, punchy, long-winded, etc.**
      Now, what I want is facts. Teach these boys and girls nothing but facts. Facts alone are wanted in life. Plant nothing else and root out everything else.
 vii. **the parts of human experience that the story will concentrate on, the themes.**
      We live in a tragic age.

Starting to hear a story (or to read one) is like looking into the future. We guess at what is to come. Here are some beginnings:

1 The tell tale heart

True! – nervous – very, very dreadfully nervous I had been and am; but why will you say that I mad? The disease had sharpened my senses – not destroyed – not dulled them. Above all was the sense of hearing acute. I heard all things in the heaven and in the earth. I heard many things in hell. How, then, am I mad? Hearken! and observe how healthily – how calmly I can tell you the whole story.

Tales of Mystery and Imagination EDGAR ALLAN POE

2 'Dad!'
'Yes, son?'
'It was Empire Day today at school. We all marched out into the playground, and each class had a Union Jack at the front. Some of the boys wore their scout uniforms, Dad, and in the middle of the playground there was a platform and one of the girls was dressed up as Britannia, with a girl each side of her in girl guide uniform. We all stood to attention while the scouts played their bugles. Then the headmaster told us all about the Empire, and how it was built by our forefathers and King George was a sort of father to all the people in the colonies, and before we came to those countries they were all savages and the kids had no boots and no schools, and they didn't know about God either. He said they're still poor but they're a lot happier now. That's good, isn't it?'

'It certainly is, son. Now I want you to get some errands for me, and then you can go out and play in the street'.

I stood waiting for the money. Suddenly I burst out:

'Dad, when are you going to get me some boots?'

Good Morning Brothers, JACK DASH (Mayflower)

3   JOHN HENRY

When John Henry was a little baby
Sittin' on his mammy's knee,
He picked up a hammer and a piece of steel, said:
This hammer'll be the death of me, Lord, Lord,
This hammer'll be the death of me.

John Henry, TOM GLAZER *A New Treasury of Folk Songs* (Corgi)

4   There was a young person from Leeds.

5   In the beginning, God created the heaven and the earth.

The endings of many stories leave you with a feeling that everything is finished — the problems have been solved or, even if they haven't, there's nothing much anyone can do about it. They all lived happily ever after — or near enough.

But other stories raise questions and doubts and expect us to think further about them.

This is one of three story cards featuring an American comic strip hero, Steve Canyon, which were put up in New York subway trains a few years ago to try to make people litter-conscious.

The Penguin Book of Comics
G. Perry & A. Aldridge (Penguin 1971.)

Different societies and different groups within the same society present very different kinds of heroes and heroines.

Every story has a moral, as Jimmy Miller, a Scots miner found out.

Jimmy Miller: Because of the way they were voting there, a fortnight later I stood for the committee. But I was still smarting a bit under what I construed to be an unjustified insult to me. And I wasn't carrying out any real trade union activity; I was just getting out of the pit and home to the boss. So I was talking in the cage, you see, with Jimmy Mercer – he's an old friend of ours – and he says to me, 'Jimmy, I don't see you,' and he spoke in a very slow, pawky Scotch way, you know, 'I don't see you in and around the pit as much as you used to do, Jim.' 'No,' I says, 'not much on now, you know, Jim,' I says. 'You've got a new delegate and you've got a new chairman,' I says, 'They'll have to do the job.' 'Ah,' he says, 'you know, Jim,' he says, 'when I was a laddie, I used to like to play at football,' he says, 'but there was only one ball and this big galoot had it and we had to let him be captain or we couldna get a game,' He says.
'So why did you let him be captain?'
He says. 'I didn't want to be captain although I was a better player than him. I didn't want to be captain; I only wanted a game. As long as I was in the team, I was quite satisfied.'
That's – I felt about the size of a mouse when I came off that cage.
Language and Class Two, Language and Class Workshop

A lot of our feelings at the end of a story depend on how we feel about the main characters, and what happens to them. There's a version of *Little Red Riding Hood* which ends with Red Riding Hood being eaten alive by the wolf. And that's it. No woodcutter comes to the rescue. No-one lives happy ever after – except maybe the wolf.

---

1 **Here's your chance to be a great detective. Look at the openings to the stories again, and then try to work out as much as possible of what the story will be like from the clues given there.**

   Take one of the openings above and continue it in the same style.

2 **Write the opening few sentences to these stories.**
   i. **a detective story about the murder of the organiser of a beauty contest;**
   ii. **a news item about the kidnapping of someone famous;**
   iii. **a piece of gossip connected with the way a teenager dresses.**

51

A new world, and a point of view

It isn't just the heroes and heroines that affect us. It's the whole world created by the storyteller. This world is made up by selecting ideas and feelings from the real world, and perhaps imagining other things, and shaping them all into a story.

Some people seem to have a bit of trouble sorting out the fact from the fiction, as the actor Bob Hoskins found out when he starred as a salesman, Arthur Parker, in the TV serial *Pennies from Heaven*:

Not everyone fell in love with Arthur whose adventures were followed by 12,000,000 viewers.

He played a sheet music salesman who seduced a school-teacher and was accused of murdering a blind girl.

"I've almost had women spitting at me in the street," said Bob. "It's silly isn't it?

"The other day I was in a local paper shop when this little old lady came up out of the blue and said 'You dirty little ——.

" 'I saw you and your antics on the telly and you with your wife and kids at home as well. You ought to be ashamed of yourself.'

"I didn't know what to do. Then the woman behind the counter refused to serve me.

"I don't suppose she knew what the other lady was on about but she probably just didn't like the look of me.'

News of the World 16 April 1978

Depending on what elements the storyteller chooses, and the way s/he fits them together, we get a sense of
   i. what that author thinks life is like,
   ii. what s/he thinks important, and
   iii. what s/he thinks is right and wrong.
These things make up the writer's point of view and are what people usually argue about, when they talk about stories.

All of these points apply to news and current events stories as much as fiction. They have heroes/heroines, a setting, and a point of view too.

Even the headlines in a newspaper tell us a lot about the world the reporters are creating, the kinds of thing they think are important. You can see this very clearly in these two headlines about the same event in April 1978:

SAFARI PARK HORROR
Kids' Corner pets fed live to Cheetahs

Sunday People

Safari Park Keepers' Strike
Morning Star

Just as important is what the storyteller leaves out. This can show us the point of view as well. For instance some people think *Coronation Street* is realistic, yet it's mostly concerned only with domestic tiffs. In real areas like that, the people have a much wider range of concerns and interests. The programme isn't wrong. People who say it's just like real life are.

1 Retell a folk tale or a fairy story that you know, turning everything upside down. Make the baddies good and the goodies bad. Make the pretty settings horrible and the frightening places comforting etc. Make sure that the ending is quite unlike the usual version.

2 Retell *Cinderella* from the point of view of the ugly sisters who believe that beauty isn't everything.

3 Write a story about someone like James Bond or the Bionic Woman or the Sweeney in which they aren't successful and get things all mixed up.

4 What doesn't exist in programmes like *Coronation Street* and *Crossroads*? Choose a popular TV series and then write out five examples of people, things, events, feelings, and ideas that would never appear in it.

5 Write a story in which characters from the world of *Coronation Street, Crossroads,* or some other well known stories take part in a very different kind of story; eg Ena Sharples as a bionic woman, Alf Garnett in a Martini advert.

6 Cut out from two different newspapers reports of the same event.

   Write down all the basic information they have in common – who, when, where, what happened.

   Write down any basic information that they do not both have.

   Look carefully at the headlines and the rest of the reports. Write down any words or phrases which give you a different impression of the event than the other report. Explain your ideas.

Limits on stories

No storyteller is a free agent. All stories are produced in a particular situation and, as a result, some stories stay unsaid. This may be simply because of the company we're in. For instance, it would be a foolish man who started to tell sexist, anti-woman stories in the presence of supporters of the Women's Movement.

Society at large sets up limits too. The British Board of Film Censors and local councils decide what films we can see. The law can be used to stop certain stories being published – as with the Obscene Publications Act in Britain.

In 1933, in Nazi Germany, Nazi supporters burned 25,000 books that they thought were anti-fascist. These included books by Ernest Hemingway, Helen Keller, Jack London, Albert Einstein, Karl Marx, Sigmund Freud, and Erich Maria Remarque (author of *All Quiet on the Western Front*)

Most published stories in Britain come from the press, TV, radio, or large publishing firms. If you're in control of any of these, you can control the range of stories that most people come across. Since 1960, seven daily or Sunday newspapers have closed in Britain. The largest had a circulation of two million readers, the smallest a quarter of a million. They didn't close because nobody wanted to read them, but because advertisers would not support them. So their way of telling news stories is not available to us now.

All stories are, in one sense, true stories. They tell us the ideas, feelings, interests, hopes and judgments of the individual storyteller and the group (or class) to which s/he belongs. Even fantasy stories do this. For instance, a lot of so-called escapist fiction contains within it a very uncritical and unreal picture of our present society. So do a lot of stories for young children.

SONG: Aren't there any families

Aren't there any families with no mum or with no dad
Or with no cars or phones or gardens of their own?
Are people always smiling? Is no one ever sad?
Has everybody got the ideal home?

Are animals always cuddly icky pretty little pets
In coats and hats and bright blue dungarees?
Do they never bite and scratch and do they never need a vet
And do they never moult or smell or get the fleas?

Do famous kings and generals win battles singlehanded?
Do soldiers never fight and die as well?
Perhaps if history books were written by the people they commanded
Wouldn't history have a different tale to tell?

And what about the dragons, lizards, monsters, kings and queens
And knights in armour doing brave and daring deeds?
Is *this* what reading's all about, cause that's the way it seems
When you first begin to learn your ABC.

Occasionally, however, there are stories which present a more critical or more real picture of people and emotions. They still have points of view.

Suddenly baby brother grabs a handful of
her hair and tugs very hard.
"Oooh," shrieks Emma –
and tears come in her eyes.

Emma's Baby Brother GUNILLA WOLDE (Brockhampton Press)

1　Imagine you have been given control over a TV channel. Make a list of any changes you would make to the advertised programmes and give reasons for your choices. Would they be whole programmes? Certain kinds of behaviour? Certain kinds of language?

2　Do you remember the first books you had in school? What were they like? Were the children in them like you? Examine a collection of children's reading books. What do the girls do? What jobs do you think the fathers and mothers in the books have? Talk about them with your friends. Do you think you would want to read them?

3　Re-read the song *Aren't there any families.* Then write a children's story which the writer of the song would approve of.

4　A lot of adverts tell basically the same story – that you'll be happy, respected, prosperous, or successful with the opposite sex, if you only buy more of the product. Cut out some figures and some settings from advertisements and write 'A day in the life of a family who believe everything they're told in advertisements'. There could be difficulties for instance, in choosing a washing powder or a pack of cigarettes.

Making a meaning

So far, it may have sounded as if only the storyteller and the story are important. But there is also the part played by us, as listeners and readers. Without us, storytellers are talking to themselves.

Because we're not all the same, we make different meanings out of the same story. Some people are shocked by stories that other people find hilariously funny, and vice-versa. This isn't because some people are awkward, or don't have a sense of humour – though it may be that! More usually, it's because we bring different viewpoints to the story, depending on our past experience. Racists or anti-racists; bosses or employees – you can't expect these groups all to have the same reaction to the same stories.

Another way of making new meanings out of existing stories occurs when we write or tell our own versions. This technique has often been used as a way of criticising our usual ideas and presenting different views. It makes people think.

Rhyme for Today

There was an old woman
who lived in a shoe
There were so many people
One shoe was too few

So she planned an extension
And ordered the wood
And laid the foundations
As all builders should.

In no time at all
The house had been doubled
It was full of a family
No longer troubled,

Because the old woman
Who lived in the shoe
Was wise and resourceful
And knew what to do.

DALE SPENDER in *Teaching London Kids 10* (TLK Collective)

---

1 Make a wall display or a class anthology or a tape recording of alternative versions of stories, carols, hymns, pop songs etc. They may be ones you already know or you can invent new ones by putting new words to some of the current hits.

2 Design a front cover for a book which contains any one of the stories mentioned in this chapter.

3 Discuss the different reactions that these people may have to the following story:
a some package holidaymakers flying out of Luton;
b the Israeli government;
c the airport security police.

Terrorist threat at top holiday airport

Security men warned last night that a busy holiday airport risks terrorist attacks. They fear that Arab guerillas could make Luton airport a target over the Easter holiday.

The warning went out when it was revealed that the Israeli airline El-Al plans to run a charter flight once a week from Luton to Israel.

Now the airport's sixty-eight security staff are threatening to strike if the flights go ahead.

They all fear that the airport will lose its low-risk security rating.

Security

Luton is Britan's top package-holiday base. And during the four-day Easter break more than 35,000 passengers will fly in and out.

A security shop steward said: 'We don't think one El-Al flight a week is worth all the risk.'

But airport manager Bernard Collins said: 'I don't think the flights will make Luton a high risk. Israeli security men will handle security jointly with us.'

Daily Mirror, 20 March 1978

5 Cold Print

The need to read and write

Beware! Be wary!
This book has been banned!
This slim volume looks like poetry,
   but it is gelignite. It will explode
   inside your head.

Monster ROBIN MORGAN (1973)

We are bombarded with print every day. Society expects every person over 14 to be able to read.

SONG: If you're looking

If you're looking for employment
Or you're reading for enjoyment
Or you're finding someone's number in the book
If you want to buy a telly
Or some fish that's not too smelly
'Cos you've found a tempting recipe to cook
If the postman brings you letters
Or you want to sue your debtors
Or you're travelling by bus or underground

It's written down, it's written down
Just open up your eyes and look around
It's no good asking passers by
The How or Where or Why
They'll say don't ask me, look it up
It's written down.

If you send a birthday greeting
Or arrange some kind of meeting
Or you're jotting down a list of what to get
If you want to claim assistance
For your day to day existence
Or to contact someone wonderful you met
If you want to keep a diary
Make an innocent enquiry
Or just make a note of certain things you've found

It's written down, it's written down
Just open up your eyes and look around
You can ask until you're grey
But you'll always hear 'em say
Use your eyeballs, look it up
It's written down.

As well as being expected to read we are expected to be able to write. Writing is not talking written down. It is a different activity. In fact talking written down may look very odd indeed. See if you can read aloud this poem and the two speeches that follow.

ygUDuh

      ydoan
      yunnuhstan

      ydoan o
      yunnuhstan dem
      yguduh ged

      yunnuhstan dem doidee
      yguduh ged riduh
      ydoan o nudh

      LISN bud LISN
         dem
         gud
         am

         lidl yelluh bas
         tuds weer goin
duh SIVILEYEzum

                              Selected Poetry e e cummings (Penguin)

Sway thing.
Kleddies n Gentlemen,
the chew-lolla gree
with mih whennay seh,
femmay coiner phrezz,
we raw linner grimment.
A nah wesher losk
Leddie Mogret to,
hosh lair sair, to
sephew words

Omster Chemmen,
lairtsin gentlemen,
thairk yoch.
War nizzen deed trooleh
quare turver whelmed.
Netch relleh wong con
tollwez biquette shore
the twonner zon the
rate poth.
Bar twommer stollwez
tretter bishaw.
Frog zomple . . .

                              Frafly Suite AFFERBACK LAUDER

Writing is better than speech for some things. It allows you to organise and structure your thoughts on the page. You can go back and alter things that seem wrong or unclear. If you wish, you can use reference books and dictionaries to help you. If you have a squeaky voice or a lisp or a stammer, none of these will be heard when your words hit the page. Christy Brown cannot speak intelligibly, is immobile and types with his toe but his words don't show this.

In a corner Mona and Paddy were sitting, huddled together, a few torn school primers before them. They were writing down little sums on an old chipped slate, using a bright piece of yellow chalk. I was close to them propped up by a few pillows against the wall, watching.

It was the chalk that attracted me so much. It was a long, slender stick of vivid yellow. I had never seen anything like it before, and it showed up so well against the black surface of the slate that I was fascinated by it as much as if it had been a stick of gold.

Suddenly, I wanted desperately to do what my sister was doing. Then – without thinking or knowing exactly what I was doing, I reached out and took the stick of chalk out of my sister's hand – with my left foot.

I do not know why I used my left foot to do this. It is a puzzle to many people as well as to myself, for, although I had displayed a curious interest in my toes at an early age, I had never attempted before this to use either of my feet in any way. They could have been as useless to me as were my hands. That day, however my left foot, apparently by its own volition, reached out and very impolitely took the chalk out of my sister's hand.

I held it tightly between my toes, and, acting on an impulse, made a wild sort of scribble with it on the slate. Next moment I stopped, a bit dazed, surprised, looking down at the stick of yellow chalk stuck between my toes, not knowing what to do with it next, hardly knowing how it got there. Then I looked up and became aware that everyone had stopped talking and were staring at me silently. Nobody stirred. Mona, her black curls framing her chubby little face, stared at me with great big eyes and open mouth. Across the open hearth, his face lit by flames, sat my father, leaning forward, hands outspread on his knees, his shoulders tense. I felt the sweat break out on my forehead.

My mother came in from the pantry with a steaming pot in her hand. She stopped midway between the table and the fire, feeling the tension flowing through the room. She followed their stare and saw me in the corner. Her eyes looked from my face down to my foot, with the chalk gripped between my toes. She put down the pot.

Then she crossed over to me and knelt down beside me, as she had done so many times before.
'I'll show you what to do with it, Chris', she said, very slowly and in a queer, choked way, her face flushed as if with some inner excitement.

Taking another piece of chalk from Mona, she hesitated, then very deliberately drew, on the floor in front of me, the single letter 'A'.
'Copy that', she said, looking steadily at me, 'Copy it, Christy'.

I couldn't.
I looked about me, looked around at the faces that were turned towards me, tense, excited faces that were at that moment frozen, immobile, eager, waiting for a miracle in their midst.

The stillness was profound. The room was full of flame and shadow that danced before my eyes and lulled my taut nerves into a sort of waking sleep. I could hear the sound of the water dripping in the pantry, the loud ticking of the clock on the mantelshelf, and the soft hiss and crackle of the logs on the open hearth.

I tried again. I put out my foot and made a wild jerking stab with the chalk which produced a very crooked line and nothing more. Mother held the slate steady for me. 'Try again Chris', she whispered in my ear. 'Again'.

I did. I stiffened my body and put my left foot out again for the third time. I drew half the other side. Then the stick of chalk broke and I was left with a stump. I wanted to fling it away and give up. Then I felt my mother's hand on my shoulder. I tried once more. Out went my foot. I shook, I sweated and strained every muscle. My hands were so tightly clenched that my fingernails bit into the flesh. I set my teeth so hard that I nearly pierced my lower lip. Everything in the room swam till the faces around me were mere patches of white. But — I drew it — *the letter 'A'*. There it was on the floor before me. Shaky, with awkward, wobbly sides and a very uneven centre line. But it *was* the letter 'A'. I looked up. I saw my mother's face for a moment, tears on her cheeks. Then my father stooped and hoisted me on to his shoulder.

I had done it! It had started — the thing that was to give my mind its chance of expressing itself. True, I couldn't speak with my lips. But now I would speak through something more lasting than spoken words — written words.

CHRISTY BROWN

When we write for ourselves we can show it to our friends or throw it away. If we write a letter it will probably be thrown away once it has been read. That's all we wanted to do – communicate. Most writing is like this. It's disposable. But writing has another use. It can be a record. In school, pupils' writing is often used as a record of their work.

Writing for exams is like this, too; it's a kind of record of what pupils are supposed to know. This kind of writing is often kept longer than our own personal kind. Writing is also used to record the successes and failures of society. Once it is written down it becomes permanent. Writing can become the permanent record of what a society wants to keep.

Instant Essay

Speed Up Your Homework!
Leave more time for Doing Nothing!
All Essay subjects covered by the World's Great Authors.
Makes Eng.Lit. a pushover.
Just look!

MY HOLIDAY
(Delete where not applicable)

This year we spent our holiday in
{ Sidcup.
Benidorm.
Tierra Del Fuego.

We were
{ staying with our gran and Mrs Dalrymple.
helping build the Hotel Majestic.   I had to share
marooned after 90 foot waves smashed our kayak.

a room with
{ Sheila
two Tour organisers.   The food was
a half-crazed Water Buffalo.
{ terrible.
terrible.
terrible.

We used to spend most of the morning
{ at Sidcup baths,
at the chemists,
in hand to hand fighting with cannibals,

then after we'd had our lunch
{ Mrs Dalrymple
a man from Leicester   would force
the half-crazed water buffalo

us to
{ wash up
push his sand yacht   until we'd
crawl on our bellies
{ got all the tea stains off gran
overtaken the man from Coventry
practically suffocated

and then if we
were really lucky we could
{ go back to Sidcup Baths.
share his sun-oil.
leap across the chasm before the crazed buffalo charged.

Unfortunately
{ we broke the diving board,
there was a chicken pox outbreak,   and we had to go
Daddy got eaten,

without supper. But it was
{ not much of a
really quite a nice   holiday, and
an absolutely terrifying

though
{ the weather wasn't too good
we all had diarrhoea   we're going back there next year.
the half-crazed buffalo killed eight of us

Bert Fegg's Nasty Book for Boys and Girls (Eyre Methuen)

This permanent record of knowledge and of other people's experience is accessible but it's not always easy for everyone to get at.

Joining the library 60 years back was, for a child, an essay in adventure. Snuffy went, nerves tensed, cap in hand, down the long, dark ramp, eased himself through the swing doors and tiptoed to the counter. Beyond, on a stool, bathed like a priest in holy calm, sat Mr Shadlock himself, deep in the racing handicap book. The boy stood for a time in respectful silence, then he sighed, sniffed, shuffled twice, coughed politely through his hot fingers, and at last, his heart pounding, he dared to put the question. 'P-please, sir, could I 'ave a joinin' form, sir?' Mr Shadlock pursued his studies. The minutes trod softly by. A gas jet belched delicately behind its frosted globe. The wall-clock tittered. Snuffy drew breath and tried again, but the words stuck in his gullet; a thin, foolish bleat threaded the silence. He blushed scarlet, licked his dried lips and turned to go. Then Mr Shadlock spoke, suddenly, violently. 'Eh?' Panic-stricken, the boy stuttered into speech. 'P-please sir, could I – could' – Like a bomb the Librarian burst among the faltering syllables. 'Out of it!' he roared.

'Didn't yer tell 'im it was for the vicar?' asked his elder sister later. Snuffy admitted the error. 'You should allus say it's for the vicar', Em' counselled, 'or for Mr Arnott at the "Duke of York", or some nob like that. It's terrible 'ard to get a form off yer own bat'. After five attempts, however, Snuffy succeeded.

The Classic Slum ROBERT ROBERTS (Penguin 1971)

---

1 **Keep a reading diary for one day – note down everything you read. Divide what you read into three sections: what you choose yourself, what teachers ask you to read, and reading necessary for everyday life. Make a table like this:**

reading done	how much	own choice	teacher's demand	necessary	was it worth it

Compare your table with your friends' and your teachers' tables.

2 **Make a one-minute tape of part of your life story or tell a story about yourself. With a group try to transcribe it accurately. Don't forget to put in all the 'ums' and 'ers' and pauses. Try to show when the voice is loud or soft and high or low. What was missed out? What about gestures and facial expressions – can they be written down?**

3 **Sometimes a logo (sign) is more useful than written words:**

Collect as many logos as you can and make a chart showing what they mean. Talk over with your friends which logos are better than written signs.

4 **Invent new logos for your favourite sport, your school, or a new ministry such as the Ministry of Humour or the Department for UFO Research.**

Different histories, different needs

Nowadays, we think it's very important for everyone to learn to read and write, to become literate. It wasn't always so. Two hundred years ago very few ordinary people in Britain could read and write. Their only chance of education was from a small number of charity and Sunday schools – if they were lucky. Reading and writing were reserved for those wealthy enough to pay for education, the lords, ladies and gentlemen.

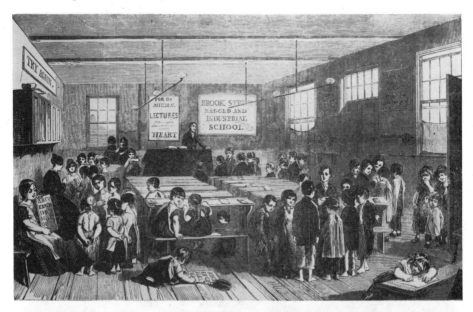

The governments thought it would be very dangerous to allow the common people to be literate. Books were dangerous. They might give people ideas. Writing was even more dangerous since writing might allow the common people to express *their own* ideas and communicate them widely.

It was the wealthy people who owned the machines and factories – including printing presses and printing works.

The *Times* was the first paper to use steam press. The press increased the rate of production from 250 sheets per hour to 1,800. By 1896 a new rotary press raised the hourly rate to 200,000 sheets.

Production of books in one year:

1810   580 titles ⎫
1850   2,600 titles ⎬   In 91 years book production increased by more than 10 times
1901   6,000 titles ⎭
1924   12,000 titles
1963   26,000 titles
1973   35,000 titles   (including 25,000 new titles)

Although in the past the common people had no access to printing presses those who could write could use this as a weapon against their masters – like this letter signed by Captain Swing, a name used 150 years ago by farm workers fighting against unemployment and low wages. ☞

As Britain developed towards an advanced industrial nation industry demanded that its workers become literate. In 1867 compulsory state education was brought in and today, a century later, most people in Britain can read and write.

> this is to inform you
> what you have to undergo
> Jentelmen if providing you
> Dont pull down your nes-
> shines and rise the poor
> mens wages the maried
> men give tow and six
> pence a day a day the
> singel tow shilings. or we
> will burn down your
> barns and you in them
> this is the last notis
> from W Sr

Our industrial society created the wealth to provide schools and books and teachers for state education. In the Third World the struggle towards literacy is still going ahead. The Cuban literacy campaign of 1961 is an outstanding example. In 1960 one in four of the Cuban adult population were illiterate.

'Next year our people propose an all-out offensive against illiteracy, with the ambitious goal of teaching every illiterate person to read and write. Organisations of teachers, students and workers – the entire population – are preparing themselves for an intensive campaign, and within a few months Cuba will be the first country in the Americas to be able to claim that it has not a single illiterate inhabitant.'

FIDEL CASTRO, United Nations 1960

A pupil was considered literate when he or she could read any of the themes chosen from the text book 'Venceromos' and write a letter to Fidel Castro, the Prime Minister of Cuba. The intensity of the final months of the Campaign were increased by some areas being declared 'free of illiteracy' by the literacy workers when their students satisfied all the requirements to be called literate. Soon the red white and blue flags 'Territorio Libre De Analfabetismo' – Land Free of Illiteracy – were flying all over Cuba and by December 1961 it was possible to claim that Cuba was, in fact, a land free of illiteracy.

Dear Comrade I Used to be Illiterate JOHN GRIFFITHS (Writers and Readers 1978).

Prime Minister, Dr Fidel Castro
I am very glad because I can read and write. Up to now I had not had the opportunity to learn and I managed this in this Year of Education thanks to the efforts made by the Revolutionary Government.

OFELIA PEREZ

Literacy in Cuba is directly connected to the lives of the people. Paolo Friere, a Brazilian, criticises reading that is divorced from people's interests in real life. Here he is describing a book used to teach adults to read:

Peter did not know how to read. Peter was ashamed. One day, Peter went to school and registered for a night course. Peter's teacher was very good. Peter knows how to read now. Look at Peter's face. Peter is smiling. He is a happy man. He already has a good job. Everyone ought to follow his example.

In saying that Peter is smiling because he knows how to read, that he is happy because he now has a good job, and that he is an example for all to follow, the authors establish a relationship between knowing how to read and getting good jobs which, in fact, cannot be borne out. Merely teaching men to read and write does not work miracles; if there are not enough jobs for men able to work, teaching more men to read will not create them.

Cultural Action for Freedom, P. FRIERE (Penguin)

It is easiest to learn to read those words most important to us, the words we really need to know. That's why everyone can read their own name and address easily and why everyone should see the need to read notices like this:

> ## SAFETY FIRST
> TO AVOID DANGER OF
> SUFFOCATION, KEEP THIS
> WRAPPER AWAY FROM
> BABIES AND CHILDREN.

T3/203

---

1 **Try to make a list of ten of the most important words or phrases a person needs to be able to read nowadays, to get about in London or another big city in Britain. Give reasons why.**

2 **Write a short simple booklet to introduce your school to first year pupils. This booklet will be given to them before they come to school. What words should they know? What should they wear? What are the most important things they should remember?**

Literature is knowledge

We tend to take books, and particularly text books, for granted as sources of knowledge and information. Anyone who can read can get hold of a printed book when it can be reproduced in its thousands. If you can *read* the words of scholars, you don't have to believe what the teachers *tell* you, about them. You can check it for yourself.

So books subvert the sort of authority which relies only on a position of power. They encourage questioning, encourage their readers to think for themselves, to form their own opinions, to gain their own knowledge.

Over the years books themselves seem to have acquired the sort of sacred authority which once belonged to teachers and priests. They have become respectable. We in the 20th century tend to think that if something is printed it must be so.

In an essay in *Knowledge and Control* the French sociologist, Pierre Bourdieu describes some different types of knowledge and ways in which that knowledge is approved by society – in other words how it is legitimised.

Serious knowledge 'High culture'	Knowledge which is becoming serious	Knowledge which is not so serious
music painting sculpture literature theatre	cinema photography jazz	fashion cookery interior decoration sport TV
approved by schools and universities	approved by critics and clubs	approved by advertising, newspapers and magazines

All types of knowledge in our society have to be approved by certain 'gatekeepers', but the gatekeepers are not always the same.

Publishers, the Arts Council, academic committees, editors of scholarly journals, these are all gatekeepers vetting knowledge before it is allowed through for you or I to make use of.

Purveyors of high culture, like schools, often feel that their clients should be protected from pop culture – they ban fashionable clothes, comics and pop records. There is a strong feeling around that reading is, in itself, a way in to high culture. Hence the stress in the popular press and in government policies on the need for *literacy*.

This movement is so powerful at the moment that any discussion of what we *mean* by literacy, what it is *for,* have been driven underground. So has any discussion of 'literacy', in the less legitimate media. It could be argued that TV and films are far more potent influences in most children's and adults' lives than books, and yet there is not much of a move to encourage the understanding and use of those media. Because they are less legitimate they are overlooked.

On Knowledge, Books and Literacy PATRICIA HOLLAND Society Today No 28 March 1978

If you want to produce and distribute your own book or newspaper nationally then of course you would need the best resources available to commercial publishers. It is possible, though, to publish your own books or newspapers for your own area, group or school. Centerprise, a bookshop and community centre in Hackney, London, has published books written by adults learning to read for other adults learning to read, books written by children for children and autobiographies of working people in Hackney – like this one by a local postman.

The actual first day I started was at Kings Cross, because I had to do two weeks at school. It wasn't bad but it was very military style. You weren't allowed to speak and if you dropped a bit of rubbish on the floor you got disciplined and all this sort of thing. You had to call the guv'nors 'Sir' and everything was done strictly to the book; you had to be there dead on time, although you didn't have to clock in; they just signed you in and you sat down and all you did virtually all day long was sort cards. On these cards you had the name of a town or city and you had to sort them for wherever it was in the country. You did this for two weeks and the last two days of the second week you had to do your test. You had to throw off so many cards, I think it was 500, in 15 minutes with no more than five mistakes. You were allowed five mistakes. The only thing I didn't like about it was travelling because I can't stand travelling to work.

KEN JACOBS, POSTMAN in *Working Lives Vol 2 1945–77* (Centerprise 1977)

All over Britain now, books like this are being produced by community publishers. And groups of people have got together to produce community news sheets and newspapers, so they can get their views across to others in their locality.

NET

85

3 October '75

THE PAPER FOR NORTH EAST TOTTENHAM

NIGHT TIME TRAFFIC BAN

ard will
iew route.

SOHO CLARION

wspaper of the Soho Society   February 1975 Vol. 2 No. 1

E:

UGH

Councillors in Soho Walkabout

dermen, councillo
ficers of Westmin
uncil Town Planni
e spent the even
nuary 14th on a
ho, visiting res
aftsmen, small f
s, shops and res
ey came at the i
the Soho Society
ncerned that cou
king so many dec
ho's future have
portunity for re
know the area,
ttle first hand
the many activi
ke place there.

e visit started
the Palace Thea
clock. After a b
action from Lesli
e visitors were
ato four groups.
members of the
ach group was con

ghty children at
aturday party at
orton Centre orga
he Soho Society i
unction with the

ABERDEEN PEOPLES PRESS

8p

Every Fortnight   № 45   Early May 1975

RIG BLOCKADE!

'Major breakthrough' as oil workers unionise

The tide is at last beg-
inning to turn for the
North Sea Oil Action Committee.

Last year, as part of their
fight to force employers to
accept unionisation of their
rig workers, they organised

A Lot of Writing

This is the way we do it:

To start with, each of us keeps a notebook in his pocket. Every time an idea comes up, we make a note of it. Each idea on a separate sheet, on one side of the page.

Then one day we gather together all the sheets of paper and spread them on a big table. We look through them, one by one, to get rid of duplications. Next, we make separate piles of the sheets that are related, and these will make up the chapters. Every chapter is sub-divided into small piles, and they will become paragraphs.

At this point we try to give a title to each paragraph. If we can't it means either that the paragraph has no content or that too many things are squeezed into it. Some paragraphs disappear. Some are broken up.

While we name the paragraphs we discuss their logical order, until an outline is born. With the outline set, we reorganize all the piles to follow its pattern.

We take the first pile, spread the sheets on the table, and we find the sequence for them. And so we begin to put down a first draft of the text.

We duplicate that part so that we each can have a copy in front of us. Then, scissors, paste and coloured pencils. We shuffle it all again. New sheets are added. We duplicate again.

A race begins now for all of us to find any word that can be crossed out, any excess adjectives, repetitions, lies, difficult words, over-long sentences, and any two concepts that are forced into one sentence.

We call in one outsider after another. We prefer it if they have not had too much schooling. We ask them to read aloud. And we watch to see if they have understood what we meant to say.

We accept their suggestions if they clarify the text. We reject any suggestions made in the name of caution.

Having done all this hard work and having followed these rules that anyone can use, we often come across an intellectual idiot who announces, 'This letter has a remarkably *personal* style.'

Why don't you admit that you don't know what the art of writing is? It is an art that is the very opposite of laziness.

Letter to a Teacher THE SCHOOL OF BARBIANA (Penguin 1973)

Here are some large pieces of work which may take some weeks to finish, so read all the suggestions carefully before you choose to do one. They all involve a lot of planning and hard work. But so did all the books, comics, magazines, newspapers etc we used to make this book. Go on – surprise yourself.

1 See if you can make a book of people's memories of your area 20 or 30 years ago. You will need to tape record a variety of people or take very careful notes of what people say to you. Shopkeepers, schoolkeepers or parents and teachers are good possible sources. Remember you will first have to make up questions to get people to talk. You must explain what you are doing and why? Once you have written up people's 'memories' show them and ask for their comments. You can illustrate you book with drawings or photographs. If you are lucky some of your interviewees will loan you photographs or you can try your local newspapers or library.

2 Make a book of war memories of people who live in your area. You will need to do the same sort of things as for task 1.

3 With a group of friends make a local newspaper. Remember it will be about your area. You will have to decide what to include and what to exclude. (What is news? Should it be about all of England, all about your town or just one street?) Is it more important to report school football matches or your local professional football club? In order to answer these kinds of questions and write your newspaper you will have to decide who you're making the paper for. Remember interesting papers are critical and controversial.

4 Write the history of your school. You will need to use both written records and people's memories. The school log book, the minutes of the education committee and your local newspaper are good sources of written information. You can also interview pupils, past pupils, staff and past staff. If your school has recently gone comprehesive it probably caused some argument or controversy. Ask the people you interview about this and any other controversial affairs that were connected with your school.

Design/print Eyre & Spottiswoode Ltd.